THE CONFUSED CONSUMER'S GUIDE

to Choosing a Health Care Plan

THE CONFUSED CONSUMER'S GUIDE
to Choosing a
Health Care Plan

Everything You Need to Know

Martin Gottlieb

HYPERION
New York

The Confused Consumer's Guide is a trademark of
Disney Enterprises, Inc.

Copyright © 1998, Martin Gottlieb
All rights reserved. No part of this book may be used or reproduced
in any manner whatsoever without the written permission of the Publisher.
Printed in the United States of America.
For information address: Hyperion, 114 Fifth Avenue,
New York, New York 10011.

Library of Congress Cataloging-in-Publication Data
Gottlieb, Martin.
The confused consumer's guide to choosing
a health care plan / Martin Gottlieb.
p. cm.
ISBN 0-7868-8233-6
1. Insurance, Health—United States—Handbooks, manuals, etc.
I. Title.
HG9396.G68   1998
368.38'2'00973—dc21   98-24775
CIP

Designed by Nicola Ferguson

FIRST EDITION
10 9 8 7 6 5 4 3 2 1

In the course of writing this book, I received invaluable help from several people I would like to thank: my editor, Jennifer Barth; Barney Karpfinger; Linda Lake; Tom Holcomb; Matt Phenix; Kathryn Shattuck; my wife, Janet Graham Gottlieb; and my sons, Graham and Ben Gottlieb.

CONTENTS

Preface ix

| 1 | The Basics: Identifying Your Options, 1
| 2 | Learning the Lingo, 14
| 3 | Identifying Your Primary Concerns, 22
| 4 | Young and Single, 48
| 5 | Women's Issues, 61
| 6 | The Best Insurance for Your Changing Family, 72
| 7 | The New World of Medicare, 85
| 8 | For the Chronically Ill, 108
| 9 | If You Have a Major Illness, 120
| 10 | Mental Health Considerations, 137

CONTENTS

| 11 | Standing Up for Your Rights, 153

| 12 | Taking Control, 165

Appendix A 173

Appendix B 211

Appendix C 241

Appendix D 249

Appendix E 251

Appendix F 261

Appendix G 265

Index 277

PREFACE

It was not supposed to be this hard.

For the better part of four decades, decent health care, easily arranged and offering unlimited choices, was a virtual right for tens of millions of Americans. If they owned their own businesses, they could pick a blue chip carrier or a Blue Cross plan at an affordable price to take care of their insurance needs. If they worked for someone else, their employers chose their health plans and covered most or all of the cost. In either case, the range of doctors and hospitals was nearly limitless.

As a result, people picked the doctors they wanted, including the costliest specialists, with little regard to price and from as wide a choice as the Yellow Pages and their friends' recommendations would allow. Same thing with hospital care. The finest hospitals in the country became accessible to people of average means. But there was a price for all this—a price in the billions, which was passed on to policyholders, employers, and the government in the form of premiums that rose extravagantly year after year for two decades.

The solution to these runaway costs is what has become the nation's new way of delivering health coverage, the broad system called *managed care*. It is an innocuous term for a complicated, transformational concept that often requires consumers to be far more involved in choosing their coverage and far more assertive in demanding what is rightfully theirs. The rewards of vigilance can be great—savings of hundreds of dollars a year and, more important, high-quality medical care tailored to the particular needs of policy holders and their families.

Twenty-five years ago there were fewer than thirty managed care plans in the country, with health maintenance organizations—their basic incarnation—serving little more than 10 million people. Today there are more than six hundred plans and, in all their permutations, they provide health coverage to more than 150 million Americans. The increase in annual enrollment regularly runs in the double digits.

Underlying this surge is a wealth of variety and complexity. Plans differ widely, yet, linking them are a few simple principles: In the purest form of managed care—in the plans known as health maintenance organizations or HMOs— each patient is assigned to a general practice doctor, often called a primary care physician. This doctor, sometimes referred to as a "gatekeeper," is supposed to take care of the patient's basic medical needs and plan a program of preventive care that includes checkups and regular tests for many illnesses. The doctor is also supposed to approve referrals for more complicated care provided by specialists and hospitals

PREFACE

also affiliated with the plan. In concept, this arrangement was originally seen as one that could starkly rearrange the delivery of medical care, from a haphazard process directed toward the crisis treatment of illness to a well-ordered one designed to preserve good health.

With ever greater frequency, however, another benefit of managed care has become its main selling point—it can save money. In theory, an organized system of care for a patient can lead to early detection of an illness and far cheaper methods of treatment. Also, in the most widely used managed care systems, primary care doctors are paid a fixed fee for the care of each of their patients, whether they require treatment or not. The idea is to radically change the way doctors are reimbursed so they don't get compensated each time they prescribe a costly high-tech treatment. Rather, the theory goes, they are rewarded for administering regular checkups and tests that can detect problems early, when they can be treated without expensive specialist or hospital care—costs that would come out of their fixed fees.

Before managed care took hold, there was broad evidence of vast overprescription of such tests and treatments—procedures that did patients no good and could sometimes exacerbate their conditions. In place of the financial rewards that led to these excesses, managed care is supposed to reward the doctor who holds down costs while helping patients. It is this benefit—clamping down on cost—that has been the great engine propelling managed care's growth.

The problems with the theory have been the great engines behind the backlash *against* managed care. They range from doctors seeing patients on an assembly-line schedule to women being pushed out of hospitals a day after having mastectomies. The incentives for doctors and plans to manage care well can also be incentives for the opposite sort of behavior, for behavior so extreme that states have legislated against some of the worst of abuses, including limits on hospital maternity stays of one day or less and gag rules prohibiting doctors from discussing with patients preferred treatments that may involve high costs to their plans. At press time, Congress was considering sweeping national legislation to deal with these sorts of issues.

An even more fundamental cause of upset is the very premise behind the HMO: the strategy of achieveing economies by limiting choices among doctors, drugs, and hospitals. Choice in just about every arena has always been a feature of American life. To limit options in something as vital as health care rubs many people the wrong way.

Adding to the sense of injustice is the fact that most people pay far more for their more limited options than they did for coverage in the expansive days of old. People who received coverage for their families through employers on average paid monthly premiums of under thirty-five dollars ten years ago, according to a survey by the consulting firm KPMG Peat Marwick. Last year, they paid an average of $127 if they worked for large companies and $175 if they worked for smaller ones.

To deal with the dissatisfaction, a variety of hybrid plans have cropped up that have fast become more popular than the no-frills HMO. Patients in many of these plans can seek care from an unlimited number of doctors without obtaining approval from a primary care physician. But they have to

PREFACE

pay higher premiums for this option, as much as seventy dollars a month or so more in some cases, and significantly more for each episode of care on top of that. Still, they wind up paying less than they would have for one of the old-fashioned plans that managed care is fast replacing. The cost of managed care plans is growing, but not nearly as quickly as that of the style of plans it is replacing.

For a vast majority of Americans, even those who don't face chronic or unusual medical problems, the system, with all its periodic irritations and limitations, can be a source of worry. A poll last year for the Henry J. Kaiser Foundation determined that for the first time, Americans were equally divided on whether the trend toward managed care was a good thing or not. Until then most people clearly favored the transition as something that could save them money while protecting their health. Too many horror stories began to change public opinion. Soon, managed care was vilified on television shows like *ER*. When the main female character in the movie *As Good As It Gets* rails against her HMO, audiences across the country reacted with boos and jeers. Yet, 80 percent of the health plan members queried in the Kaiser Foundation poll rated their own care as satisfactory.

For all the bonafide public policy concerns and rough edges that come with managed care, it is clear that for the vast majority of Americans who are fundamentally healthy, the system seems to work well enough. It can lower bills, eliminate paperwork, and provide for a pattern of care that encourages individuals and families to monitor and protect their health rather than turn to a doctor only when they are sick. Above all, for the smart consumer, managed care, at

PREFACE

least in a great majority of cases, can provide appropriate medical care at a relatively modest cost.

The purpose of this book is to help you make knowledgeable decisions about your health care coverage. These can not only save hundreds or thousands of dollars over a year but can also assure you the degree of quality care and flexibility you want. To do this, the book will explain the often numbing jargon that has attached itself to this field and offer simple checklists of questions for you to ask and research. At the back of the book is a compilation of statistical information about more than three hundred health plans, which will help you distinguish one from another.

In the coming chapters, you will also learn how others in situations similar to yours have come to make their health insurance decisions, people like the Casons and the Stewarts of upstate New York who, when faced with their own health coverage quandary, breathed deeply and took charge of the situation. You can do the same. And you may find, as they did, that the best course is nothing that you could have predicted when the search began.

THE CONFUSED CONSUMER'S GUIDE

to Choosing a Health Care Plan

| 1 |

THE BASICS: IDENTIFYING YOUR OPTIONS

For Steve Stewart, a small businessman in the rural town of Stone Ridge, New York, the dilemmas of the nation's health insurance system seemed to play out with regularity in his own life. For several years through the '80s, he had relied on a traditional policy from his local Blue Cross plan for his family coverage. The plan was similar to the vast majority bought by Americans at the time, a *fee-for-service* policy that allowed him to go to any doctors and hospitals he wanted. Each year, Steve and his wife, Fern, had to pay the first $500 of their bills, the portion that is known as the *deductible*. Once the deductible was met, they also had to pay 20 percent of each bill, the portion of the bill called the *co-payment*. These standard features cost the couple hundreds of dollars a year on top of their *premium*, the regular monthly fee that is a standard payment for all health insurance. Meanwhile, the yearly cost of their premium was steadily rising, from $1,560 in 1984 to more than $1,850 in 1987. And they began to notice that the plan placed individual ceilings on what it would pay for specific treatments, regardless of the actual cost. At one point, this left the family with a $600 reimbursement on a $5,000 medical bill. Their total medical costs were usually more than twice as high as their basic premiums. "It was a rip off," said Fern. Professional craftspeople who make high-end pottery, Fern and Steve had little margin to cover the escalating health care costs that seemed to be hitting them from every direction.

They thought they found their answer in the alternative of managed care. A company called the Mid-Hudson Health Plan had made dramatic inroads in the Hudson Valley region by offering monthly premiums of under $250 for a family of four with no history of serious illness. True, the monthly premiums were a bit higher than the Stewarts had been paying (which is usually not the case for managed care plans). But it was easy for them to see managed care's true monetary allure; in place of the deductibles, 20 percent co-payments, and coverage ceilings that the Stewarts had to contend with on the old Blue Cross plan were simple and minimal extra charges. The co-payment for doctor visits was a flat three dollars. The payment on every prescription was also only three dollars. As a health maintenance organization, it restricted the doctors the Stewarts could see, but this, it turned out, was not to be a hardship. Among the doctors affiliated with the plan were those already used by the Stewart family. On top of this, Fern and Steve felt comfortable with the idea of a system that stressed regular checkups, tests, and other forms of preventive care. "The theory appealed to me," Steve said recently. "The idea of concentrating on keeping people well seemed to be the way things ought to be structured."

Before long, however, problems—significant problems—began to crop up. Annual premiums at the plan, called Well Care in later years, rose, from $2,607.96 in 1988 to $3,016.44 the following year, and $3,621.24 the year after that. By 1995 the Stewarts were paying an annual premium of $6,317.47. In a phenomenon paralleled in millions of families across the country, the figure seemed all the more astounding when compared to the premiums of barely a decade earlier. The Stewarts were paying more than four times as much as they first did on their old Blue Cross plan in 1984.

The family's dissatisfaction did not stop with price, however. As with many other plans, the effects of fast growth began to manifest themselves in many ways. Well Care didn't pay its bills on time. Invoices for tests and hospital services went unpaid for as long as eight months and, along with the higher premium notices, the Stewarts received a growing collection of dunning letters for payments that didn't fall under their responsibility.

Again, the family's experience was far from unique. Sloppy management and organizational turbulence have been a bain of the managed care explosion. With rigorous state and Federal regulation just beginning to take hold, any number of operators have tried to turn a profit through corner-cutting and worse. A spokesman for the company maintained in an interview that the extent of the company's service problems had been "vastly exaggerated"—a point disputed strongly by Steve Stewart and many of his neighbors. In any event, Well Care's entire management team was replaced in 1996 amid government investigations. The company eventually agreed to pay a $91,000 fine for violations of state insurance regulations.

THE SEARCH BEGINS

The mess left the Stewarts looking for a health care plan once more, but this time, they had some help. Around the corner, the Cason family was in the market, too. Dave Cason had decided to leave his job of fifteen years and start up his own business, a tool and dye company that serves the plastics industry. Continuing to carry the fee-for-service policy that had been provided by his last employer was a problem, though. It simply cost too much money—close to $500 a month for his family of four. So the Casons and Stewarts teamed up and sought out a health plan together.

"First thing," said Dave, "we eliminated Well Care from consideration." Almost everything else was in contention, though, because with Steve and Dave in business for themselves, their selection was not limited in any way. While many employees of middle- or large-sized firms might have a choice of two or three plans—or no choice at all—the Ca-

IDENTIFYING YOUR OPTIONS

sons and Stewarts hit the Yellow Pages and came up with more than a dozen plans serving their area. As they began making calls, they analyzed what was most important to them through winding conversations that encompassed their past experiences and the particular health needs of family members.

Price and quality of care ranked high, of course, but other priorities included the proximity of family doctors they liked and their ability to choose the best hospitals and specialists without restriction if a family member became seriously ill. The last determinant led them away from signing on with a health maintenance organization in favor of other types of managed care companies that offered greater flexibility. For the Stewarts and Casons, freedom of choice was worth the extra $100 a month and the higher co-payments that allowed them to go beyond the doctors and hospitals affiliated with a plan when making their medical choices.

These sorts of plans are known variously as *preferred provider organizations* or *point-of-service plans*. Behind the jargon and subtle differences between the two lies a simple principle: A plan member can see a doctor registered with the plan for a small co-payment, usually between five dollars and fifteen dollars a visit. But if the member goes outside the plan or sees a specialist without the approval of a primary care doctor, the co-payment rises to between 20 and 50 percent of the bill, a figure that could run into three figures or more. And the patient usually has to deal with the sorts of medical forms that members of pure HMOs have gratefully bid good-bye.

Deciding that the wider choice plans were the way to go

was one hurdle for the Casons and Stewarts. They then had to narrow the list of plans in this category. They called the plans' agents and invited them over for talks, a practice far more prevalent in smaller towns than in big cities. Some of the agents were disconcerted to find two families at the table when they had assumed there would be just one—the idea of four adults probing for unanswered questions seemed to some of them almost like cheating, Steve recalled. "We told them they have to take or leave both of us," he said.

What emerged through the visits and an analysis of the informational brochures the salespeople left behind was a clear pattern. Several plans offered lower premiums than the others, but their deductibles and co-payments were higher. When the families balanced out the different financial aspects of the plans and matched them against the family medical histories, it seemed that they were all within the same ballpark—less than $100 a month separating them. If the families had lived in a big city, the cost differences would have been more extreme. There a pattern often emerges in which some plans pay better compensation to better credentialed doctors and higher quality hospitals and pass on the cost to plan members through higher premiums. Meanwhile, another tier of plans offers lower premiums by striking deals with less expensive medical providers.

Dave's wife, Donna, did a bit more research. She poured through directories provided by each plan, which listed their affiliated doctors by medical specialty and where their offices were located. In several of the plans, the closest primary care doctor was in Poughkeepsie, a city forty minutes away on the other side of the Hudson River. She eliminated

IDENTIFYING YOUR OPTIONS

those immediately. More promising were the ones that listed doctors in Kingston, the closest big town, twenty minutes away. One by one she called the doctors listed and found, as many other health plan members have, that the impressive lists of affiliated doctors were not as impressive as they appeared to be. In a large number of cases, the doctors had accepted a certain number of members from a particular plan and closed their doors to any more.

One plan whose price was right and whose doctors were still accepting new patients was Blue Cross/Blue Shield of Northeastern New York, which offered a special rate to small businessmen through a local chamber of commerce. While about 10 percent better than the other rates, it was still more than $1,000 higher a year than the rate for a pure HMO, which didn't allow for the freedom of choice the families wanted. Now the question was, Was there a way to lower the Blue Cross rate further?

Here, Dave and Donna did some arithmetic and began to chart the differences between plans measured against their family's health history. They noticed that the cost of a plan fell with a rise in the deductible—the amount of money the family paid out of pocket for each individual's medical costs before their insurance kicked in. They computed their health care costs for an average year and for a year in which they sustained a lot of bills. They matched it against the Blue Cross plan with the highest deductible—$2,500 instead of the usual $500. For a policy with a $500 deductible, the monthly premium was $380.67. For a policy with a $2,500 deductible, the monthly premium dropped to $273.76. Because both families hoped to use doctors on the plan panel, limiting the co-payment for doctor visits to $10, they figured the high deductible would only become a factor in a catastrophic year. "I found that in the worst case year the cost was a wash," Dave said. "In an average year, I came out substantially ahead." That is, even in the worst year—when he severely fractured the bones in his upper arm—the cost of the family's medical care with the $2,500 deductible would have been about the same as the cost with the lower deductible but the higher premium payments. The advantage to the high deductible option became evident to the Casons: In most years, the family would have come out ahead, sometimes by a few hundred dollars. So, the choice for the Casons and, after a few conversations, the Stewarts, was clear and unexpected: go for the plan with the highest deductible.

They thought through one last point before closing the book on their health insurance decisions. With a high deductible, they knew they were leaving themselves open to the risk that in a particularly rough medical year, they would be exposing themselves to up to $2,500 in unbudgeted costs in addition to whatever co-payments they would incur for doctors or hospitals unaffiliated with the plan. A protracted hospital stay would inevitably cost the family at least $2,500. To guard against that large a hit, each family decided to bank the roughly $100 in savings per month they would achieve by paying the premium on the policy with the $2,500 deductible rather than the higher one for the $500 deductible policy. "In three years, if we don't have to draw on the money, we'll have enough in the bank to cover us even in the worst year," said Dave.

It took the Stewarts and Casons a full six months to re-

IDENTIFYING YOUR OPTIONS

STEWART FAMILY WORKSHEET

INSURANCE CHOICES	PREMIUM-YR	MED. COSTS	AFTER CO-PAY	TOTAL COST
None	None	2,755	2,755	2,755
HMO	3,600	2,755	320	3,920
POS ($500 deductible, all care in plan)	4,888.04	2,755	320	5,208.06
POS ($500 deductible, half care out of plan)	4,888.04	2,755	380	5,268.06
POS ($2,500 deductible, all care in plan)	3,285.12	2,755	320	3,605.12

search their decision, building a knowledge base from the ground up. For many people working for larger companies, there is less of a need to dive into an undertaking this extensive. For one thing, the largest employers in the country do a lot of research for their workers, not only dispersing informational literature and answering questions one-on-one through their benefits departments, but undertaking and publishing employee polls that reflect which plans are thought of most highly.

WORKING FOR A BIG COMPANY

For the millions of people in the employ of medium- to large-sized companies, there is still the same need for reflection and analysis. Marilyn Timbers passed up the opportunity eleven years ago to take several other jobs that paid a bit more money in order to go to work for Xerox in Stamford, Connecticut, where she runs a gamut of programs that include assistance with elder care, child care, college tuition, and adoption. Her husband, John, had left a large law firm that the family received its health insurance through and set out on his own. The couple decided it would be best if Marilyn could find work at a blue chip company with excellent benefits that could cover the couple and their five children—the cost and quality would be far more attractive than anything John could find as a single practitioner. And the Xerox plan was all they could have hoped for—comprehensive and inexpensive.

But in 1994, the company, like other large ones around the country, augmented its plan, which was escalating in cost dramatically, with a number of managed care alternatives. Xerox, like other companies, was so committed to getting its employees to convert to managed care it offered monetary incentives for them to do so. For Marilyn and her family, this presented real, and at first overwhelming, choices. "A lot of materials came out, to some extent almost too much from each of the HMOs," she recalled.

The information base has only grown over the years. In addition to the material from more than a half dozen competing companies, Marilyn and her coworkers now receive information developed by Xerox—a poll measuring worker satisfaction and fact sheets comparing price and indicating how long the plans have been in service, whether they have been accredited by the ranking rating agency, what their physician turnover rate is, and what hospitals they are affiliated with. Initially, when faced with the decision to choose between plans, each of the alternatives seemed attractive be-

IDENTIFYING YOUR OPTIONS

cause they were far cheaper than the fee-for-service plan that Xerox continued to offer.

In the end though, price was only one factor in the family's decision-making process. In fact, the Timbers wound up choosing a plan called PHS that, when they first enrolled, was a couple of hundred dollars more a year than the other managed care plans, but was appealing in qualitative ways. It included almost all the family's doctors with the exception of one of Marilyn's, and it offered a rare benefit: It allowed specialists to be seen without referrals from primary care doctors. With the family brood nearing teenage years, there was a steady need for dermatological care and quick access to orthopedists for sports injuries. "Time is probably the most precious commodity any of us have," she reflected. "The reason I liked PHS was they don't have the gatekeeper." Further, she said, "I know the doctors and I like the way they're set up. I'm willing to pay a few hundred dollars more for this. Then I look at price."

Last, she said, she made it a point to review the supporting material provided by Xerox. If the plan had drawn a low satisfaction number on the company poll, or if it sustained a large disenrollment rate among doctors, she would have taken another hard look at it. But it hadn't, and what's more, its cost over the years has dropped below that of competing companies. As her children move into adulthood without having experienced any significant medical mishaps, Marilyn pronounced herself happy with her decision and the care received through the plan.

Many of the exercises she and the Stewarts and Casons

THE CONSUMER'S GUIDE TO HEALTH CARE PLANS

undertook are ones that you can learn from. Some are self-evident—at least in retrospect. Others reflect the nuances of a new and ever-changing health insurance marketplace.

[1] *Trust your experiences and those of your friends;* ask about the reputations of health plans and think about the service you receive before looking at a plan a second time.

[2] *Determine the two or three most important qualities of a plan for you and your family.* For the Stewarts and Casons, the flexibility to choose from the widest range of doctors and hospitals surpassed even their fundamental desire to lower their medical costs. The proximity of plan doctors counted for a lot, too. For Marilyn Timbers, the opportunity to see specialists without going through a primary care doctor ranked high. For other families, just as reasonably, cost will be paramount, or the desire to continue a relationship with a longtime doctor, or a plan's reputation for paying bills promptly and answering members' questions quickly and accurately.

[3] *Double-check what seem to be even the most indisputable facts offered by a plan.* Donna found, as many people do, that phone book–sized directories of plan-affiliated doctors mean little if few of them are accepting more plan members as patients.

[4] *Do comparison charts for your insurance options to determine the costs you would incur, running the numbers for best case, worst case, and average circumstances.* You'll

IDENTIFYING YOUR OPTIONS

be surprised at the differences. Make sure to keep in mind whether you anticipate major expenses, such as pregnancy or a planned surgery. And remember that in the great majority of circumstances, you will be locked into your choice for a year before you can change to another option. By balancing the low premium payments of some plans against their higher deductibles and co-payments, Dave was able to determine that what seemed to be gaping differences were in fact relatively minor differences in cost. By analyzing the effects of a high deductible policy, he was able to come up with an unconventional alternative that promises to save money.

[5] *Always measure the features of a plan against your particular medical needs.* Blue Cross of Northeastern New York crystallized as an option when Dave matched its cost features against the real medical experiences of his family. Marilyn found the extra premium cost of PHS well worth the access to dermatologists and other doctors her children relied on. For people with chronic medical problems or mental health needs, the importance of scrutinizing the particulars of a plan are even more pronounced.

| 2 |

LEARNING THE LINGO

To engage in a process similar to that of the Casons and Stewarts may seem intricate enough, but add one further complicating factor: You have to analyze some complex information written in what amounts to a foreign language. This is the language of health care, where nothing that can be said in down-to-earth lay terms is ever conveyed that simply. Jargon has built up over the years in ways that tend to cut out the public and leave important information to the realm of the insurance and health care industries. Understanding even the most basic terms offers you a window into

LEARNING THE LINGO

the thinking behind the choices presented to you and the opportunities they may present.

Until the past few years, the type of health coverage that was the norm around the country was called *fee for service*. This dense term describes an arrangement, still very much in use, in which an insurance company pays a fee to a doctor or hospital—they are often called *providers*—each time they provide care to one of the company's policyholders. The policyholders pay for this service in three ways. They pay monthly *premiums* that cover the price of the policy and are often subsidized to some degree by medium- and large-sized companies. They pay *deductibles*, the first several hundred, or even few thousand dollars, of medical costs before insurance reimbursement kicks in. And they make *co-payments*, typically 20 percent of every doctor and hospital bill, with the insurance company picking up the remainder.

Fee-for-service care has dwindled in the face of the managed care revolution. Where 87 percent of the private health insurance provided in 1982 was fee-for-service coverage, a dozen years later it counted for only 12 percent, and the proportion continues to fall. Managed care, which in one form or another now accounts for more than 90 percent of private health coverage, has spawned a terminology of its own. The term *managed care* itself is open to some interpretation, but generally covers a broad array of plans that, unlike fee-for-service arrangements, contractually link insurance companies with doctors and hospitals. In place of fee-for-service arrangements, where policyholders—sometimes called *consumers*—can choose providers as they wish, managed care plans require members to choose from among their affiliated doctors and hospitals or provide strong economic incentives for them to do so. By the way, when you choose a managed care plan, you are no longer referred to as a policyholder. You are called a *plan member*. On the business end of managed care, you are referred to by a less warming term. You are a *covered life*. As a covered life, you can be covered in a few different ways. Here's a breakdown of the names they go by and the characteristics they offer.

Health Maintenance Organizations. Although the term *HMO* is often used interchangeably with "managed care," it actually refers to a specific type of plan that embodies managed care principles in their purest form. HMOs should appeal to consumers most interested in value for the dollar because their premiums tend to be lower than other types of plans and members pay a small fee, usually between five and fifteen dollars for doctors' visits and almost nothing for hospital stays. The reason for the value is that HMOs are the most restrictive of managed care plans. They require all members to use doctors and hospitals affiliated with the plan; those that, in the lingo, are on the plan's *panel*. And your access to these providers is restricted further still.

In HMOs, each member chooses a *primary care physician*, generally an internist or family practitioner whose job it is to coordinate their patients' coverage and handle as much of it as he or she is capable of. A plan member can see a specialist or use a hospital only after receiving a referral from a primary care doctor. In this way, the plans can enforce

LEARNING THE LINGO

treatment norms and preventive medicine practices that can keep costs down. And they can drive hard bargains with doctors—particularly primary care doctors—by paying them a fixed fee for the care of their patients, no matter how often they see their individual patients or how costly their treatment becomes. These fees are called *capitation rates*. They usually work out to provide far less compensation than the individual bills doctors collected under the old fee-for-service medical insurance system.

Fortunate are those patients whose doctors are affiliated with plans they want to join. They can enjoy the savings HMOs bring and continue their relationships with their doctors. But even in cases like these, the drawbacks to the HMO concept can present themselves. With their income from each individual visit down, doctors often try to pack two or three appointments into the time they used to reserve for one. One result is that for many patients, their doctors may be the same, but their relationship changes.

The fundamental drawback of HMOs, however, is more serious. Should significant illness strike, an enrollee must use the doctors and hospitals affiliated with the plan or pay for medical costs out-of-pocket. If the leading specialist in town is across the street from where you live but outside the plan's panel, you are almost certainly out of luck; the cost for regular visits with a nonpanel doctor is overwhelming for most people. For the young and healthy, this may be a remote concern. And the budget-conscious may well be satisfied that other quality doctors are represented on a plan's panel. But for many people, this cost of joining an HMO is simply too high. For these people there are options outside of classic HMOs and they are becoming the most popular in the health care universe.

Point of Service. This type can cost as much as $100 more in monthly premiums than traditional HMOs, but offers complete freedom of choice of doctors and hospitals. Costly spin-offs of pure HMOs, *point of service options* require members who use the doctors and hospitals affiliated with the HMO to pay the small fees extended to the HMO members. But whenever they want, they can also seek care from providers unaffiliated with the plan. The price for this, however, goes beyond higher premiums. For service outside the plan's panel, each member must pay a deductible, which according to the consulting firm KPMG Peat Marwick, on average comes to more than $350 a year. Furthermore, as in fee-for-service plans, they must make co-payments. But where fee-for-service co-payments normally run to 20 percent of the bill, in point-of-service plans, it usually runs to 30 percent of the bill and can sometimes rise to 50 percent, depending on the arrangement offered by the plan at the time of enrollment.

Preferred Provider Organizations. Point-of-service options are one way that health plans try to meet a public desire for more freedom. Another is a closely related type of plan called a preferred provider organization. Here, networks of providers contract with plans and agree to see members at discounted rates. They often do not use primary care physicians as gatekeepers, so members can also visit specialists without needing approval. Also, members can normally go outside the plan's providers for care, although this option is far more expensive, with more costly co-payments replacing the small fees for providers affiliated with the plan.

Staff Models, Group Models, and Other Styles. For those who find the HMO option attractive, however, there are other choices, reflected in further terminology. Most plans are business enterprises, frequently publicly traded, and based on the idea that tough entrepreneurial practices can save money and streamline care. But there is a strong *not-for-profit* core in the industry that includes many of the oldest plans, like Kaiser Permanente, which started in Northern California fifty years ago. When it comes to the for-profit plans, some people are troubled by what they see as an inevitable conflict between the provision of the best medical care and a need to grow profits for investors. Others, however, believe, first, that even plans that are nonprofit face similar pressures and, second, that there is enough fat in the medical care system for plans to turn profits and deliver quality care at the same time.

This said, it was uncanny how many times the most innovative, patient-helpful initiatives encountered while researching this book came out of a handful of the not-for-profit companies. Among the standouts were the Harvard Pilgrim plan in New England, Group Health Cooperative of

THE CONSUMER'S GUIDE TO HEALTH CARE PLANS

Puget Sound in Washington State, and the Kaiser empire, which, despite highly publicized disputes in California, is still thought of highly by most members and benefits managers. Like most plans, many of them have at times encountered bouts of bad publicity for some of their policies and decisions, but they still have managed to preserve good reputations.

A second division in the way HMOs are organized involves whether they employ their doctors and own their hospitals or contract for services. The *staff model* HMO is exemplified by the northern California Kaiser plans. In these, doctors hired by Kaiser provide care in Kaiser-owned clinics and hospitals. While some consumers bristle at the lack of options and uniformity of coverage, others appreciation the one-stop service the clinics afford. Primary care doctors, specialists, lab tests, and pharmaceutical services are all available under one roof. Potentially more important is the ability of staff model HMOs to better develop disease-management plans that involve doctors and nurses who work directly for them and hospitals they own.

More prevalent today are *group model* HMOs, which can offer some of the same convenience. Here, HMOs contract with large group practices of doctors to provide care, usually on an exclusive basis, in their large and multifaceted offices. Primary doctors, specialists, and lab tests are often available at one site. Plans also contract with individual doctors who care for members in their own offices and often belong to several plans. These alignments are called *individual practice associations.* Most plans rely heavily on these relationships, combined with nonexclusive contracts with groups of doc-

LEARNING THE LINGO

tors. Together, these linkages, in addition to those with hospitals, form the plan's *network*.

A last bit of basic terminology concerns the drugs that a plan approves for reimbursement. These are delineated on an approved list of drugs called a *formulary*. The formulary can change regularly as new drugs are approved by the Federal Food and Drug Administration, cheaper *generic*, or non-brandname, drugs come on the market, research confirms the preferability of certain drugs, and the plan shops among manufacturers for the best price. If you regularly use a drug, it is important to find out whether it is listed on the formulary of a plan you are considering.

As with any language, a basic familiarity allows at least simple conversation to occur. More important, it allows users to ask questions. The fundamental questions you ask, more than anything, will determine how successful you are in arranging the care you need in the most economical way.

| 3 |

IDENTIFYING YOUR PRIMARY CONCERNS

What are your most important health care concerns? Obviously, you want the best care. But how important is low cost to you? Proximity to doctors and hospitals? The ability to change physicians when you want? Each of these priorities leads to other relevant questions, as they did for the Stewarts and Casons and Marilyn Timbers. It is these questions, which when well answered, make the difference between an informed choice about health insurance and one that might leave you short of dollars and the kind of care you seek. The questions you ask, on the one hand, should be almost self-evident and on the other should reflect the complexities of

IDENTIFYING YOUR CONCERNS

a health care system in transition as it relates to the particularities of your life.

The health care market is a competitive one. If you and your family are in relatively good health, every managed care plan in your area wants your business. Many will answer your questions at informational meetings, frequently held at larger companies and, for Medicare recipients, at neighborhood restaurants. Don't be afraid to call a plan and ask its sales representatives for information you think will help you make a decision. If the plan can't or won't provide you with the information, there may be legitimate reasons for this, but if other plans seem willing to answer your questions, you might think again about the plan that can't. There are also informational resources outside the plan, some of which are reflected in this book's appendices. Ratings agencies and state agencies frequently compile important information, as do large employers, who sometimes develop their own analyses of plans and their employees' evaluation of them.

THE BASICS

When considering a health plan, start simply by reducing the myriad of issues that you might entertain to a few uncomplicated basics:

Does the plan offer the quality of medical care you seek, including access to doctors you have come to depend on and trust?

Does it offer a competitive price?

Does it provide easy access—through location and ease of appointments, among other things—to care?

Does it provide straightforward and authoritative assistance through phone help lines?

Does it influence its affiliated doctors to hold to their appointment schedules so that you will not be kept waiting inordinate amounts of time after arriving for a visit?

Is it financially secure, with a track record of reimbursing doctors and members in a timely manner?

Does it act more as an ally than an adversary when you are trying to secure high level care?

Next, take stock of all the resources available to you as you try to find answers.

INFORMATION SOURCES

What do your friends and coworkers have to say about their experiences with the plan? Their answers might open up a wealth of considerations you hadn't anticipated. You might well expect accounts of the quality of the plan's doctors but wind up hearing more about how long a wait your coworkers put up with before getting medical appointments or how long they have had to wait to be reimbursed for their bills. This should be an indication that concerns you haven't thought of might be everyday facts of life for members of the

IDENTIFYING YOUR CONCERNS

plan—facts of life you might find annoying, or worse, if you joined.

What is your doctor's opinion? This can be one of your great resources. Beyond the fact of whether your doctor is affiliated with the plan, his or her views can be insightful on such matters as the plan's general reputation in medical circles, the quality of its doctors, the ease with which referrals to specialists are granted, the availability of quality drugs on the plan's formulary, and the reputation of its affiliated hospitals. The doctor may also be able to shed light on a piece of the plan's underlying economics, which can be a prime determinant of quality: how it reimburses its affiliated physicians. If it skimps, plan members suffer in two ways—the best doctors stay away and the others have an incentive to churn patients through their offices perfunctorily in order to maintain their incomes.

In one of the most notorious HMO practices, doctors in many plans were prohibited, through what came to be known as "gag clauses" in their contracts, from talking to patients about how they were compensated and in some instances about treatment alternatives to those covered by the plan. The uproar was so great that some plans voluntarily withdrew these clauses and many states legislated against them.

There are two general methods of compensation for doctors: *a per visit payment* (and the doctor should be able to indicate whether it is a fair one or not) and *capitation*. Under capitation, doctors receive a fixed monthly payment for the care of each of their patients. The payment is supposed to cover the cost of almost any care provided by the doctor. The theory behind capitation is that it will encourage doctors to perform regular checkups and tests so that potentially costly illnesses will be identified and nipped while they are still cheap to cover. In this way, a doctor can, in effect, increase his or her income, since less of the capitation fee will be used for medical expenses. But a low capitation rate can lead to problems for plan members, which start with a tendency for some doctors to see large numbers of patients for short periods of time.

Because of its monetary incentives, capitation also encourages primary care doctors to treat many conditions that under the old fee-for-service form of coverage they would have referred to specialists. In many cases this makes a lot of sense. Excessive treatment by specialists was one of the forces behind out-of-control medical inflation. But today there are, without a doubt, cases of primary care doctors taking on cases that should really be in other hands. How can you determine this? Although you should always keep in mind that your doctor's view might be colored by antipathy to managed care in general or one plan in particular, he or she can still be your best resource. Your doctor should have a professional's knowledge of whether the plan's reimbursement structure provides enough compensation for a physician to perform optimally or not.

How is the plan rated by independent accreditation agencies? The industry standard is the National Commission on Quality Assurance (NCQA), a nonprofit organization in Washington with employers, consumers, health plans, and labor unions represented on its board. It issues accreditations of one and three years to health plans, depending on

IDENTIFYING YOUR CONCERNS

how many of its standards they meet; on occasion they deny outright accreditation to plans whose quality level is severely lacking. The NCQA also publishes detailed analyses of plans (some of which are listed in the appendix), which can be obtained by calling 202-955-3500 or checking the organization's web site at www.ncqa.org.

Does your state insurance department issue annual reports ranking plans by such categories as price, member and doctor disenrollment rates—that is, the rate of people who leave the plan—and consumer complaints? In New York state, for example, the insurance superintendent publishes an annual survey that shows certain plans proportionally drawing consistently higher levels of complaints and complaints sustained on appeal than other plans. The HealthNet HMO sponsored by Empire Blue Cross and Blue Shield, with $196 million in premiums in 1996, generated only five complaints to the department that were upheld. NYLCare Health Plans, with $136 million in premiums, generated forty-one upheld complaints during the same time period. Its complaint ratio was ten times greater.

Has the health-oriented magazine Health Pages *analyzed insurance issues in your area?* It has in more than twenty states and its surveys often turn up striking disparities in cost and services among plans. For information, call *Health Pages* at 212-505-0103 or check its web site at www.healthpages.com. Some local consumer groups also make an effort to measure local plan performance. The granddaddy of these is the Center for the Study of Services, which offers involved analysis of plans, largely based on surveys of Federal employees, particularly in Washington, D.C. and the San Fran-

THE CONSUMER'S GUIDE TO HEALTH CARE PLANS

cisco Bay Area. Copies of the center's analyses can be obtained by contacting the organization at 733 Fifteenth Street NW, Suite 820, Washington, D.C. 20005, calling 202-347-7283, or at the web site, www.checkbook.org.

Have you made use of all the information offered by your employer? Across the country, the largest companies not only provide substantial information about the plans they offer as choices, but in some instances rate the plans and offer monetary incentives for workers to join the ones considered not only best in terms of price, but quality also. General Motors and GTE are leaders here. GM, for example, not only has its own surveyors evaluate the plans, but subsidizes employee choices in proportion to how highly rated the plans are. A company employee who chose a top-rated plan for family coverage last year paid only nineteen dollars a month in premiums. An employee who chose a poorly rated plan paid a monthly premium of $175. This is the most extreme example of company involvement in health plan choice, but scores of other companies offer advice through benefits officers and such supporting material as satisfaction polls of company workers.

If you work for a smaller company that has not undertaken its own analysis of health plans, find out if there are corporate health policy consortiums in your area that have completed ratings. Organizations such as the Pacific Business Group on Health in San Francisco and the Washington Business Group on Health, each supported by local employers, publish their findings on HMOs and other health plans.

IDENTIFYING YOUR CONCERNS

QUALITY

How many of the plan's doctors are board certified in their specialties? Doctors achieve board certification after taking extra training in their specialties and passing a rigorous examination. Even generalists, including primary care doctors, can be board certified. There is nothing to say that a doctor who isn't is not highly competent, but certification is a professional yardstick that you should consider seriously. (You can find out if a particular doctor is board certified from the doctor's office, the plan, or the American Board of Medical Specialties at 847-491-9091.) Most plans compute the proportion of their affiliated doctors who are board certified. Ask the plan for this information. They make it available to rating agencies, large employers, and state agencies. Periodic recertification is becoming standard in many specialties as well, and plans should be able to provide this information about specific practitioners. Ask, too, how often and under what circumstances the plan encourages the use of nurse practitioners and physician's assistants in place of doctors. This is appropriate for many routine procedures, but should be done only with patients in general good health and with a doctor readily available as a backstop.

How many of the plan's hospitals are teaching hospitals? These are the few hundred hospitals across the country where young doctors are trained by many of the best practitioners in their fields. They are generally considered the highest quality hospitals with the most cutting-edge equipment and the most prestigious medical staffs. Other hospitals in your area no doubt also have high-quality reputations.

See which get good marks, particularly in specialties that are of particular concern to you, in studies conducted by local business groups, and in national surveys, like that undertaken annually by the magazine *U.S. News & World Report.*

How does the plan rank in independent surveys of its members, like the annual Federal government poll of tens of thousands of public workers covered by managed care companies? Also telling are the responses by members of various plans to the standardized poll administered by the National Commission on Quality Assurance. Each of these polls asks large numbers of members pointed questions about how satisfied they are with their medical care and other aspects of their plans' service.

Disregard the results of surveys commissioned by the plans themselves. They invariably show widespread member satisfaction, in no small part because of the way questions are framed and the poll sample is selected. The NCQA survey, by contrast, is administered by a third party with no affiliation with any plan.

What free preventive services does the plan offer? Many provide annual physicals, mammograms, pap smears, flu shots, well baby visits, and some other inoculations for adults as well as children. The best also screen for colon cancer and cholesterol.

What percentage of the plan's members avail themselves of these services? This information provides a good indicator of how serious the plan is about taking care of the health of its members through testing and prevention. Plenty of plans claim commitment to preventive measures of medicine, but the proportion of members who have received these ser-

IDENTIFYING YOUR CONCERNS

vices suggests otherwise. In these cases, it is most likely that the plan touts the services as a marketing come-on but does not organize or promote them to its members in a way where they can make a substantial difference. Again, you can often receive information about what free services a plan offers and how many members make use of it from state insurance or health departments, the NCQA, your employer, or the plans themselves.

If the plan says it offers special treatment programs for illnesses, are there any measures available that indicate how successful they are? Several plans, for example, say they have programs geared toward treating juvenile asthma, which can be a very expensive disease if it results in frequent admissions to the hospital through the emergency room. Many professionals believe that if well managed, the illness should never result in an emergency room admission. Can the plan produce independent data indicating what its rate of emergency room admissions is and how it has changed over the years? These sorts of measures are first being developed and computed now and should become more and more available in the near future.

COST

How does the plan's monthly premium compare to others? If you are considering a number of plans, make a chart that begins with a listing of the premiums and leaves room for other economic and coverage variables.

What does the plan offer in exchange for an attractive price?

Particularly it is important to check whether the coverage includes items that may be of express value to you, but that only certain plans may include in their package. Among these are items like home care, such medical equipment as diabetes kits, and drugs that you take on a regular basis.

How do other costs match up among the plans you are considering? If you are looking at a point-of-service option that allows use of doctors and hospitals outside the plan panel, you must meet a deductible and make co-payments on these visits. How high is the deductible for the plan you are looking at? What proportion of the doctor or hospital charge will you have to cover as a co-payment? Depending on the plan, these can run from 20 to 50 percent of the bill. And in many plans there is another expense that many members don't realize until they join. Many plans set a dollar limit on what they will cover for different kinds of medical services. If a doctor or hospital bill comes to more than this, the plan will only pay toward its maximum limit called the "reasonable and customary charge" (minus the co-payment). The plan member is left to pick up the rest.

For example, let's say your plan sets a limit of $100 on payment for a well baby visit and requires a 30 percent co-payment from members who use doctors not on its panel. Your pediatrician is not affiliated with the plan and charges $120 for a well baby visit. Because of the ceiling established by the plan, you wind up paying fifty dollars for the visit, rather than thirty dollars—thirty dollars for the co-payment and twenty dollars to make up the difference between the plan's maximum limit and the actual bill. For members in

IDENTIFYING YOUR CONCERNS

most large cities where doctor bills are high, these ceilings become a real factor in increasing your cost of care. It is worth asking plans if they have payment limits and what they are for routine checkups, flu treatments, and other visits that your medical history tells you you might be making.

How do a plan's co-payments, deductibles, and other costs compare with competitors'? If you are contemplating joining a traditional HMO, there are differences in co-payments, even if you can't go outside the plan's panel for care. The cost of a visit to a doctor can vary from five to fifteen dollars. In point-of-service plans, the variability in co-payment can

---

WHAT'S THE TRUE CO-PAY?

Many health plan members wind up paying far more for individual doctor visits and other services than they expected. The reason is that their co-payments are based not on their actual medical bills, but on what their plans consider the "reasonable and customary charges" for the services they obtained. In this case, a member whose plan advertised a 30 percent co-payment paid nearly 42 percent of the doctor bill out-of-pocket:

Doctor's bill for treatment for bronchitis:	$120
Plan's reasonable and customary charge:	$100
Member's co-pay at 30 percent:	$30
Uncovered part of bill:	$20

Member's total out-of-pocket expense: $50, or 41.6 percent

be far more dramatic. Also, find out what proportion of the cost of a prescription you will pay.

Is there a limit on how much reimbursement the plan will make to hospitals in a year or during your lifetime? Some plans have limits of half a million dollars and others of $2 million. Still other plans have no limits at all. Some plans will put a limit on the maximum number of hospital days they will cover in the course of a year. If you have a chronic condition or a family history of cancer or heart disease, it is worth perusing the fine print to see if the plan you are leaning toward might ultimately come up short.

Like the Stewarts and Casons did, try to approximate what the cost for a plan would be when the premium is added together with such other items as deductibles and co-payments. Try to estimate what the cost would be in an average year of medical use and an extreme one, based on your family's health care history. For example, add the cost of twelve months of premiums to the cost of likely doctor visits, using the small co-payment for doctors affiliated with your plan and, if you choose an option other than a strict HMO, the higher co-payments outside the plan. Then, if you regularly use unaffiliated doctors or hospitals, add the deductible or the part of the deductible you believe you are likely to use up based on past history. The differences can run into the hundreds of dollars in many typical cases. But if plans are roughly comparable in terms of cost, other distinguishing qualities will assume greater importance.

IDENTIFYING YOUR CONCERNS

CONVENIENCE

How many primary care doctors affiliated with the plan are located within a reasonable distance of your home or office? Again, be sure to check whether these doctors are still accepting new patients from the plan. And make sure you distinguish between different plans offered by the same company. For example, the large Oxford company operating in New York, New Jersey, and Connecticut offers one plan called Freedom and another called Liberty. Each has different doctor panels. Often doctors in the area don't even know about the distinction, considering themselves members of the "Oxford" panel. You could sign up for one plan and find your doctor on the other—clearly out of your reach no matter how close he or she is.

How difficult does it appear to arrange timely appointments with your doctor of choice? How long can you expect to wait to see the doctor once you arrive for your appointment? Will you get the time you need for your examination and diagnosis, or will you feel rushed? If you are deciding whether to join a plan with a doctor you would like to use, ask the doctor's receptionist how far in advance you will have to arrange appointments. A good benchmark for acceptability is the one established by General Motors: Appointments for urgent situations, such as high fever or persistent diarrhea, should be available in two days or less. For such less urgent conditions as sore throats, headaches, or colds, appointments should be available in two to four days. Routine visits, for blood pressure tests, follow-up checkups and the like, should be available within two weeks of your call. Annual physicals and other well care visits should be available within a month.

Once you make an appointment, you may face a particularly annoying delay—a long wait past your appointed time in the doctor's waiting room. If you can, visit the doctor's waiting room before making a decision and find out firsthand if people have been stuck there for hours. If you don't have the time, ask friends who use the doctor. Independent patient satisfaction surveys of plans almost always ask members if they have experienced long waits. Some plans score uniformly poorly in this regard.

How close is the nearest drugstore that accepts prescriptions covered by your plan? And how close is the nearest hospital affiliated with the plan that you would want to use?

What is the plan's policy about emergency room care? Does it pay only for care arising out of what, after diagnosis, is deemed to be a "true emergency"? Or will it also pay for care from an episode that did not turn out to be an emergency, but that a plan member could have reasonably thought was an emergency at the time of treatment? Chest pains, for example, may turn out to be caused by little more than heartburn. But as a mounting number of states have determined, a person who has experienced a heart attack is probably using good judgment in racing to an emergency room if the pain appears unusual and frightening.

Legislative efforts in many states require plans to pay for care that a "prudent layman" would identify as an emergency, regardless of the outcome. In this instance and many others where state legislation would seemingly regulate the behavior of your plan, you may still be out of luck when the hos-

IDENTIFYING YOUR CONCERNS

pital bill arrives. Under Federal legislation, plans that are self-funded by companies are exempt from state regulation and come under the generally looser jurisdiction of the Federal Department of Labor. Because many medium- to large-sized companies fund their own plans, in California and other states the largest number of health plan members falls outside the purview of the pertinent state laws. If your company's plan is self-funded and exempt, you may still have options to choose a plan that does fall under state law. Many large companies offer other plans in addition to the one they sponsor and fund themselves.

How long do you have to wait to get answers over the phone from a plan representative and how reliable is this information? It is worth trying out a prospective plan's customer service line. Frequently the wait for someone to simply pick up the phone can be extensive and the lack of clear answers to questions about reimbursement and covered services can be alarming.

How lengthy and convoluted are reimbursement forms, and how long does it take to get payment? For members of pure HMOs, these questions are moot. One of the great conveniences of HMOs is the lack of forms and the straightforward payment mechanism—for the most part just a few dollars paid to a plan doctor at the time of a visit. But for the majority of managed care plan members—those involved in arrangements that allow them to see doctors who are not affiliated with the plan—the reimbursement process can be time-consuming and frustrating. The mistakes made by plan personnel can seem downright idiotic and can take months to rectify. State insurance departments often track which plans receive inordinate numbers of complaints by category, including delivery of inaccurate information from plan representatives.

Does your plan allow easy use of unaffiliated hospitals when you are traveling and outside the plan's general service area? Particularly if you travel a lot because of your work or as a family leisure activity, check the plan's policy on reimbursement for care far from home. Some of the most bitter disputes between members and their plans involve reimbursement for out-of-state emergency room visits at unaffiliated hospitals. At the least, if at all possible, have someone call your plan for you if you are headed for the ER.

FLEXIBILITY

Does your plan allow you to switch primary care physicians? How often? The importance of your primary care doctor is obvious in a managed care arrangement. Your plan should help you switch doctors when the fit is bad, but some plans allow only one change per year. This may not allow room to maneuver, particularly if you are dealing with an unexpected illness.

Does the plan provide reimbursement for second opinions? In this more rigid system of medicine it is particularly important for patients to validate the medical advice they receive. Many plans will allow for an additional opinion in serious medical cases.

Does the plan permit you to choose a specialist as your pri-

IDENTIFYING YOUR CONCERNS

mary care doctor? For many people, a specialist should be the primary care physician. If you are suffering from a condition that needs regular, specialized attention, this specialist in fact becomes the center of your health care team. Several plans have begun to allow such specialists to assume the primary care role that traditionally is reserved for family doctors and other generalists. Many women prefer to choose an obstetrician-gynecologist as a primary physician. The plans that allow wider access to specialists provide an incalculable benefit to members with particular needs because the standard method of HMO operation for such people can become extraordinarily burdensome.

Most plans require members to receive approval from a primary care physician for every visit to a specialist. For those with chronic conditions, this is obviously a frustration and inconvenience.

In the overwhelming number of cases where specialists are not the primary care doctors, does the plan allow members to see specialists without prior approval? As mentioned earlier, this is generally permitted in the plans called preferred provider organizations. Some traditional HMOs are also beginning to allow such visits on a limited basis where the specialist is affiliated with the plan. In a growing number of cases, plans are allowing primary care doctors to grant multiple referrals to specialists for patients who will obviously need a higher level of treatment on several occasions over a period of time.

SPECIAL NEEDS

As the last two questions imply, there are millions of Americans with special health needs that oftentimes are difficult for standard issue health care plans to meet. Probably the greatest proportion of HMO horror stories develop out of situations that are more complicated than those faced by most people whose routine health needs can usually be successfully accommodated through primary care doctors and managed care norms. Other people may simply prefer different styles of medical treatment than are the norm. Take stock of your special circumstances and plan with them foremost in your mind.

Does the health plan limit coverage of "preexisting conditions"? Preexisting conditions are health problems that have developed prior to the time a person joins a plan. Many plans refuse to provide coverage for these conditions from anywhere between ninety days and two years. The intent of this provision is to protect plans from being joined by people a few days after they receive an unfavorable diagnosis. But they can leave you without coverage for your most important health care needs. The Kennedy-Kassebaum health care bill of 1996 plugged one gap in this regard. Large numbers of people who leave one job through which they received health care coverage are now entitled to automatic coverage through a new employer regardless of their preexisting conditions if the company offers insurance to its workers. But huge numbers of people are still vulnerable to exclusion from coverage because of the condition of their health. Here is one example: A person leaves one job where the company

IDENTIFYING YOUR CONCERNS

provided insurance and obtains another where the company does not. The person tries to buy insurance privately but finds he cannot because insurers can still consider a preexisting condition and reject the application for coverage.

Does the plan offer enough highly qualified specialists who are expert in your particular condition and who are still accepting new patients? Has it developed a disease management strategy for your particular illness that involves coordination between different specialists and, where applicable, the use of other professionals, like physical therapists? And is the best local hospital for your treatment needs on the plan's list of affiliates?

Does the plan limit the number of hospital days it will cover in a year? If you have a history of long periods of hospital treatment, it is important to know whether plan benefits may run out before you are likely to complete your cycle of care.

If you have been using a particular drug, is it listed on the plan's formulary? Often, in an effort to save money, formularies list generic versions of brand-name drugs or alternatives that are supposed to serve the same purpose as costlier drugs. Many patients have complained, however, that these alternative drugs simply do not perform as well as the ones they replace. If you are very reliant on a drug you have used for many years, it may not be worth giving it up to save a few dollars on a less expensive health plan.

If you are a believer in alternative medicine therapies, does the plan cover more than just the least expensive nontraditional medical procedures? Does it cover, for example, acupuncture or allow you to choose a practitioner of holistic medicine as your primary care doctor?

What does the plan offer in terms of mental health services? For people used to seeing therapists for the regular problems of life, managed care can be a jolting experience. Usually payment is limited to a small number of visits for a defined problem. Lengthy treatments on a therapists' couch or extended group therapy sessions fall outside the reimbursement criteria of managed care plans. For those with more extreme mental health needs, managed care plans generally provide coverage through specialized subcontractors, called *carve-out companies*. They are referred to this way because the mental health component of care is "carved out" of the coverage plan and assigned to the subcontractor. For those with a need for these services, the identity and track record of the carve-out company is crucial to know. You can join a health plan with a sterling reputation, but if its mental health subcontractor is a poorly run operation with no record of quality, you could suffer unfortunate consequences. And even if you do your background research, your work may take you only so far. Some health plans have changed subcontractors so frequently that there is no guarantee the company in place when you sign up will remain there.

Still, how the company provides coverage for your condition is something to be studied in detail. It is also essential to know what kind of drugs it allows, how much hospital and group home coverage it permits, how extensive its coverage of therapy is, and how flexible it is in meeting needs established by complicated, shifting conditions.

If you have been diagnosed with HIV or full-blown AIDS, are

IDENTIFYING YOUR CONCERNS

there doctors in the plan with wide training and experience in this area and can the plan outline a coordinated treatment program involving many specialists working in conjunction with each other?

If you are having difficulty getting pregnant, does the plan cover not only testing and relatively low-cost drug therapies, but higher cost procedures, such as in vitro fertilization, that you may want to try?

What is the plan's policy on reimbursing expensive cutting-edge procedures that are often the last hope for people with serious illnesses? A persistent matter of dispute between many plans and their sickest members is the plans' refusal to pay for procedures they deem "experimental" even after affiliated doctors recommend them. Bone marrow transplants, for example, are procedures that are increasingly recommended by doctors when all else has failed in remitting cancer. But they are typically considered experimental treatments by most plans and therefore outside the scope of coverage. Appeals of rejections of coverage have sometimes won reimbursement for patients with conditions where the transplants are deemed to have had a reasonable rate of success.

PERIPHERALS

Deciding which health insurance package to choose is the core decision you will make about the medical treatment you and your family receive. But there are other issues and decisions that are important in their own right. When considering your health care needs, don't fail to look into these other areas:

[1] *Dental and vision coverage.* Most companies only offer one option and in each case the option has generally become less attractive with the passing years. Large companies traditionally contributed as much as fifty dollars a month to employees' dental plans, but more recently employees have generally been asked to contribute a portion of the cost. Co-payments also add to employee costs. An emerging alternative are dental HMOs, but there are relatively few and waiting lists are usually quite long.

[2] *Disability coverage.* This is not strictly speaking a form of health coverage, but it can prove invaluable if you are out of work for health reasons for an extended period of time. Short-term disability is provided by most employers and usually provides up to 60 percent of a worker's pay for up to three months, or sometimes six months, after an incapacitating accident or illness. These policies are often used to cover pregnancy and maternity leaves, generally of up to ten weeks. Long-term disability insurance kicks in at the expiration of short-term policies. Some companies provide long-term coverage as well, but more and more consumers have been buying their own policies, either because their employers don't offer this coverage or because they want to augment their company benefits.

IDENTIFYING YOUR CONCERNS

    Under most plans offered through employers, the insurance makes up from 40 to 60 percent of your salary for long periods in which you are incapacitated. Most experts recommend you arrange coverage for at least 60 percent and ideally 70 percent of your salary. Insurance companies are hesitant to go beyond this point, fearing that they would be removing an economic incentive that would hasten your return to work. Differences among policies are subtle but significant and should be studied in detail. Some benefits are tax free while most are taxable. Some benefits are paid out through a beneficiary's lifetime; others for shorter periods. Women must pay higher premiums than men, because it has been determined actuarily that they make more use of disability insurance than men. But many experts agree that the insurance is well worth considering. For people between thirty-five and sixty-five, the odds of a disability lasting more than three months are three times greater than the chances of dying.

[3] *Long-term care coverage.* This is insurance that helps finance nursing home care and other types of extended care, like assisted-living units. In some cases, it also reimburses home health care costs and the expense of home attendants for people who can no longer care for themselves. The number of long-term care plans is considerable and coverage varies widely in terms of cost and choice, with the differences often obscure to the layperson's eye. So beware. If you anticipate hav-

ing reserves that you don't want to exhaust on long-term care needs, this insurance can be invaluable, but issues that have to be studied in detail include relative cost, what services will be reimbursed, whether your policy is protected against inflation, and whether you lose all benefits if you let the policy lapse, even after ten or twenty years.

Your employer may offer long-term care insurance, but probably will require you to take on the entire premium expense yourself. Federal tax breaks that went into effect at the beginning of last year make these policies more attractive, but they still can be problematic because of the high cost of nursing home care. If the reimbursement, particularly on lower cost policies, barely makes a dent in the average nursing home care bill in your region, this kind of policy may not be a wise investment.

[4] *Flexible spending accounts.* These are arrangements in which pretax dollars are deducted from your paycheck and placed into an account that can be used to pay a wide variety of medical expenses not covered by your health insurance—co-payments, deductibles, contact lenses, and drugs. Because your account is made up of pretax dollars, your buying power escalates considerably, but with a catch: Any money left unspent at the end of the year is nonrefundable. It is turned over to the Federal government. Careful conservative planning in predetermining the size of the account and creative ideas about how to spend the money in it should guar-

IDENTIFYING YOUR CONCERNS

antee that you, and not Uncle Sam, are the beneficiary of the funds you have set aside.

[5] *COBRA.* If you leave your job for any reason, this benefit can be immensely helpful to you. The acronym stands for the Consolidated Omnibus Budget Reconciliation Act of 1983 and refers to the specific provision in it that allows workers to extend the health coverage they and their families were receiving on the job for up to eighteen months. You must pay the full premium yourself, plus a 2 percent fee, but the coverage can sustain you through a period of joblessness, while you are setting yourself up in your own business, or even for a while after you begin a new job with inferior health benefits. Even if you decline the benefit for yourself, dependents who received coverage under your plan are still eligible for COBRA insurance extension—a provision that can be immensely helpful if, say, they have pre-existing conditions that are not covered by the plan offered by your new employer.

| 4 |

YOUNG AND SINGLE

Chuck Wojnowski, now thirty-eight, has spent an average of two years on a job, changing health plans and doctors with each move. He is single and in good health. When he took a job last year at Southern California Edison, one that he plans to build into a career, he was presented with a half dozen choices for health coverage—pure HMOs, other kinds of managed care plans that allowed visits to unaffiliated doctors and hospitals, and even traditional fee-for-service coverage. Offered this range of options, most Americans, according to numerous surveys, would choose something other than the cheaper but more restrictive HMOs. As people adjust to the new world of health coverage, it is clear that if they can afford it, they prefer to pay the extra dollar for the opportunity to choose from the widest variety of specialists, hospitals, and general practitioners.

But for millions of people, the standard HMOs, however restrictive in choice of doctors and hospitals, still make the most sense, in no small measure because they are cheaper—often forty dollars or more a month in many parts of the country. For the most part, these people are very much like Chuck. They are younger. They are healthy. And they are single. As they see it—correctly—the chances that they will need expensive medical care are slight. Chuck, for example, has seldom had to see a doctor for anything other than routine physicals, with the exception of one outpatient surgery procedure. He didn't see the need to pay more for a point-of-service plan because he figured it was unlikely he would need specialized care, or any sort of complicated medical care. And, actuarially speaking, as a currently healthy man under forty, he was right. He chose Kaiser of Southern California.

Of course, there are still health concerns that can lead people like Chuck to plans other than the least expensive. Primary among them is the desire to keep a relationship with a current doctor. But for many younger people, or those who have moved around a lot, these relationships simply don't exist. They didn't for Chuck. "I've never established a relationship with one doctor," he said. When it comes to health plans, he added, "For me, it's more about price than doctor choice." Adding to the validity of such a strategy is a bit of reflection on how the overwhelming number of people pick their doctors; it is usually through the casual recommendations of friends or the proximity of a doctor's office to a home or a workplace. These are hardly guarantors of first-rate medical care. A more deliberate choice from the panel of a high-quality HMO can often lead to a far sounder selection of doctors.

Financially, too, there were additional reasons that lured Chuck to the HMO option. Aside from lower premiums, he liked the idea of dispensing with co-payments and deductibles, which can save him hundreds of dollars over a year. Also attractive is the lack of paperwork. He pays five dollars a visit and fills out no forms when he sees a doctor. "When I started working, I had an indemnity plan at first," he recalled, referring to the traditional fee-for-service type of insurance. "As soon as HMOs were available, I started using them—they were so easy."

SIMPLE IS BEST

In many quarters, there is a strong belief that in years to come, the classic, restrictive HMO will give way to plans with point-of-service options. But it is clear that Chuck can serve as a representative for the millions of Americans for whom the standard HMO works just fine and will continue to do so. When he had to make his choice at Southern California Edison, he asked co-workers their preference and found most talked in terms of favored doctors rather than favored plans. But when it came to plans, he said, Kaiser emerged as a clear favorite. It also happened to be the one with a hospital closest to his house. His decision seemed easy.

While saving money, HMOs give these people—younger, healthier, and often just starting out in the job market—what they really need: inexpensive regular checkups and, if a plan is chosen wisely, a safety net of decent care in case a health need arises. If your company is still offering fee-for-service plans, there is another plausible option to consider, a policy with an exceptionally high deductible of $2,500 or more. These sorts of policies are commonly referred to as *disaster* or *catastrophic coverage*. The cost of such policies is far less than that for coverage with a standard $500 or $1,000 policy. And, if you are in good health, the chance is slight that something will strike that will rack up costs in the thousands of dollars. But the chance remains. And the cost can mount for checkups and care for such routine ailments as sports injuries and allergies. This is why membership in a classic HMO is probably a better way to go.

THE LOSS OF FREEDOM

True, you will have to give up the freedom that has caused many Americans to seek their health care outside of HMOs. You will be confined to choosing among the doctors and hospitals on the plan's panel. Your primary care doctor will have to authorize all your referrals to specialists and may have a monetary incentive to avoid making such referrals. The drugs your doctor can prescribe will be defined by the plan formulary.

Should serious illness strike, these limitations may seem all the more objectionable. They can limit you from seeking out what you consider the optimal providers and treatments. But given the statistically slight chance that such illness will occur, these limitations, particularly for the budget conscious, are worth the risk, if the choice is made wisely.

At the beginning it is worthwhile to take stock of the medical care you currently receive. Do you have a primary care doctor you find satisfactory? Do you rely on a specialist regularly for a recurring condition, like allergies? Do you take drugs for any conditions that are particularly effective? Is there an area hospital that you believe to be the one you would call on should the need arise? When looking at an HMO, it is important to consider how many of these resources would be available through the plan. Then you will face the personal decision about what you are prepared to lose in exchange for lower cost. To ensure that you analyze this fully and make the wisest choice among HMOs, there are a number of steps to follow.

[1] *Fully understand the restrictions entailed in HMO coverage.* From the vantage point of good health, limited choice of hospitals and required referrals from primary care doctors for all specialist visits might seem peripheral issues. And if your current doctor is on a plan you select, the range of other available doctors might seem irrelevant. Yet, a small change in circumstance can make these issues major. Consider the case of Roy Moore, a machine parts inspector for Boeing Aircraft in the Seattle area. As a union shop steward, he was

very familiar with the health coverage program worked out by the company and the International Association of Machinists. It would reward workers who left the company's expensive fee-for-service plan for HMOs with cash payments of $600 in the first year of the new program and an additional $400 and $200 in the next two. Roy, who is single and thirty-eight, took the bait, switching from the Kings County Blue Cross Blue Shield plan to the Blue Cross HMO called Selections.

But it wasn't long before he came to regret the decision. An old sports injury acted up, causing him to visit the chiropractor he had come to rely on. This time, however, the chiropractor would not see him under the plan's coverage without a referral from his primary care physician. When he called his primary doctor, whom because of generally sound health he had seen only intermittently, he discovered that he had moved—forty-five miles away. So he scrambled for another primary care doctor, calling two recommended by the doctor who had moved. Both doctors, it turned out, were accepting no new Boeing Selections referrals, having filled the proportions of their practices they wanted to allot to the plan. Roy tried three or four other doctors before he found one reasonably close to him who could write him a referral.

While the doctor examined him thoroughly, recommended exercises, and provided the referral to his chiropractor, Roy says he's switching back to the fee-for-service Blue Cross plan and passing up the chance at the additional $600. The delay in care cost him time, he said—days when he was in pain. "I want to go to specialists without necessarily being referred," he said. "I think because of all the red tape and the hoops you have to go through, it's a turn off to get medical attention. Losing the convenience and losing the control is not worth the monetary gain you think you might have."

There are many HMO members who have had different experiences, or who might think that the dollar savings are worth these sorts of disruptions. It is useful to ask yourself if you would be one of them in circumstances similar to Roy's. It is worthwhile, too, to remember that HMOs have led the way in trying to make medical care less costly. For many, this has meant checkups and doctor visits that seem to be far more rushed than they did in the past and surgery that often entails far less hospital time than before and that in many cases is done on an outpatient basis. Even an HMO adherent like Chuck Wojnowski has, quite literally, felt the difference. A few years ago, while being covered by an HMO, he had a painful varicose seal operation in his groin area, which was done on an outpatient basis. "The one complaint I have is that they don't allow you time to heal," he said. "I was in unbearable pain at home for three days."

Would his operation have been undertaken on an outpatient basis regardless of the type of coverage he had? Perhaps, but then again, HMOs have been at the forefront of stripping inpatient care to a minimum, so much so that state legislatures have outlawed childbirth procedures without overnight stays and mastectomies with stays of under forty-eight hours. That such legislation is necessary is a testament to how hard HMOs strive to limit costly recuperative time in hospitals. As fit as you might be, this could be a factor someday in how you are cared for if some sort of surgery is needed.

[2] *Make sure the potential plan you are considering is well-established, well-regarded, and meets your needs.* You want a plan that has a panel that includes the best doctors and hospitals in your area and has earned a strong reputation for customer service. Again, one barometer of quality doctors is the percentage of board certified specialists. As mentioned earlier, if plans you are researching can't or don't furnish you this information, call your state insurance department to see if it tracks this information. More directly, ask friends and co-workers for recommendations not only of doctors but of plans. This is what Chuck Wojnowski did before making his choice. If a choice between a couple of plans is still too close, look into the fine print. Does each plan offer unlimited hospital coverage or are there annual and lifetime dollar limits on covered care? Do either of the plans limit your number of specialist consultations over a year or, conversely, does either allow primary care doctors to make multiple referrals to the same specialists during a single visit for conditions that require protracted care?

Does one spell out an appeals process for coverage denials more clearly and expansively than the other?

Differences among plans do not stop here. There are questions about how plans manage their own affairs that have direct implications on patient service and care. A plan in poor financial condition, or one that is poorly organized and late in paying doctors and hospitals, is a poor foundation on which to build your medical care. With late payments, doctors can become disaffected and, consciously or not, give their patients shorter shrift. They may also decide to leave the plan if getting reimbursed is not worth the hassle of paperwork and late payments.

In the turbulent and changing world of health care, even the best-looking plans can turn out to be shaky. In the tri-state area of Connecticut, New York, and New Jersey there was no more highly rated company than Oxford Health Plans, but last year the company ran into serious problems. It was unable to pay doctors on time or realistically predict what it cost to deliver the care it promised.

Short of doing a deep financial analysis of a plan, it is best to go with companies that have stood the test of time and have substantial revenues and access to capital through the stock market or their own reserves. For the layperson, the best way to get information about this is from the plans' promotional literature and a call to your state insurance department, which can provide basic financial information and, in some cases, industry financial ratings.

As mentioned earlier, if you work for a large company, you may be able to avail yourself of another resource. Many large companies poll their employees on satisfaction with their health plans and publish the results. In many regions of the country independent business groups, like the Pacific Business Group on Health in San Francisco, publish their own ratings. State insurance departments can also provide you with additional information. This can often include how many consumers and providers have left a plan in the course of a year—a clear measure of dissatisfaction—and how many members have filed complaints about a plan, and how many of these have been substantiated.

[3] *Go beyond friends' recommendations and board certification to review a plan's list of doctors carefully.* Don't simply pick the practitioner located closest to you or the one that a friend said something nice about. Convenience can be a factor, but as you survey the roster of primary care doctors, choose a handful and call them up. See if they will make time for a visit and a conversation. Look around their waiting rooms. Have people been kept waiting a long time past their appointments? Do you feel good about the surroundings? Try to assess the doctor's manner. Ask about things that are important to you—whether he or she truly encourages regular checkups and preventive testing, and their opinions on issues such as the ready use of medication and alternative medicine techniques.

And don't be shy about asking the doctor about the

health care plan you are considering—do they pay relatively well compared to other plans and do they pay on time? These issues may help determine how much time you will have with the doctor and how devoted to you he or she will be. Ask whether the plan readily accepts referrals the doctor makes to specialists and whether it has denied treatment options that he or she has recommended.

Most important of all, find out how the plan pays its providers, whether on a per session basis or a capitated basis. If the doctor is paid through the standard HMO method of capitation, there is a built-in incentive for the doctor to avoid referrals to specialists or even frequent follow-up visits. Pressing this point, ask, too, if the doctor is eligible for any bonus payments at the end of the year if treatment costs are held below a certain level. This is another lever that plans use to try to dissuade doctors from what they would argue is the needless overuse of tests, specialists, and medications. You may have another idea about whether much of this treatment is needless. Remember to investigate the plan's list of specialists if you have a recurring condition that has led you to visit specialists in the past.

At the bare minimum, when calling doctors make sure they are still accepting appointments from members of the plan you are thinking of joining. Often physician directories published by plans are thick with the names of doctors who have agreed to affiliate with a plan, but who accept only a limited number of members.

YOUNG AND SINGLE

[4] *Be sure to check out a couple of other basics that could be important to you.* If you take a drug regularly for a long-term condition, be sure the drug is on the plan's formulary and at least ask the plan how often it deletes drugs for replacement by others. If there is, at least by reputation, an exceptional hospital in your area—typically a teaching hospital with senior board certified doctors and cutting-edge equipment—make sure it is listed on the plan panel. The chance you will be using it may be slight, but if the occasion arises, it will be reassuring to know that the hospital will be open to you and the great bulk of your bills will be reimbursed. Beyond this, it is a clear indication of plan quality. There are plans that are suspected of avoiding affiliations with hospitals expert in complicated conditions, because these conditions are expensive to treat. Without the hospital affiliations, the plans stand less of a chance of attracting costlier members.

[5] *Always carry insurance.* There are more than 40 million Americans without insurance, mostly because they can't afford it. A disproportionate number of those without coverage are young working people who could afford a plan membership, but who simply don't believe they will incur an illness serious enough to jeopardize their finances. An additional incentive to forgo insurance is the practice of many companies to offer employees a cash rebate if they decide not to buy into any of the coverage options that are extended. The rebate is meant as an inducement to people who

can be covered under a spouse's plan. For a person with an entry level salary, it sometimes serves as another inducement to pass up insurance entirely. It never pays to go without insurance, which by its nature is meant to protect against unlikely and unanticipated events. For young people who find it hard to imagine becoming sick, the word "unanticipated" has a particularly remote meaning. Never underestimate how frequently the remote can become real.

| 5 |

WOMEN'S ISSUES

When Christine Needham of Boston first looked for an HMO ten years ago, she settled on the Harvard Community Health Plan, traditionally one of the most highly regarded in the country. She was looking not only for herself, but for the three other employees of a fledgling company called Cityshopper, which publishes a shopper newspaper distributed around Boston. "I called up every plan I could think of and they seemed to be the one most interested in small businesses," she recalled. "They were competitive on price and they listed a lot of doctors and good hospitals in our area. And they were always friendly on the phone."

Nine years later, when Christine became pregnant, what she wanted from a health plan became more involved. The youngest of five daughters, she learned from her sisters' experiences and decided that she wanted a childbirth as natural and drug free as possible, but in a quality hospital in case complications arose. For her, this meant using a midwife rather than a doctor not only for the delivery but for the care leading up to birth.

Harvard, like many other plans, over the years had come around to accommodating requests like this. When Christine became pregnant a year earlier in what eventually terminated in a miscarriage, the plan offered one midwife and four obstetricians in the clinic closest to her house, but the midwife was not permitted to perform the actual delivery. By the time Christine was pregnant again, a midwife named Shirley Kamarowski had been transferred to the plan's Copley Center clinic and given the green light to deliver babies. The result for Christine was a healthy boy named Morgan Franklin and a sense that at this important moment in her life, she received the kind of care she wanted through a health plan that acted as ally rather than adversary. "They were always so helpful—any question I had, I got answered," she said. "And Shirley was great. Midwives, they work with you, they don't tell you what to do."

Not every woman would want her baby delivered by a midwife and without drugs. But having the ability to choose what she wanted was critical to Christine. And after years in which many of their most inflexible and egregious policies toward women triggered public outcries, many health plans

WOMEN'S ISSUES

are making efforts to become more accommodating. At their worst, managed care plans were refusing to pay for more than a day—or sometimes more than eight hours—in a hospital after childbirth. Mastectomy patients were sometimes forced to check out in equally short time. The situation became so extreme that at least fourteen states legislated against what came to be called "drive-through deliveries," and President Clinton called for national regulations.

Perhaps with this in mind, several plans have tried to develop policies and practices that are more responsive to women's needs. Instead of relying exclusively on primary care doctors to coordinate coverage, some plans have changed their policies so that obstetrician-gynecologists can assume the gatekeeper role. A handful of plans allow oncologists to serve as primary care doctors for women who have experienced mastectomies or other bouts with cancer. As Christine found, the acceptance of midwives is on the rise, a practice, by the way, that can also be financially advantageous to health plans. And almost every managed care plan offers free tests, including pap smears and breast exams, designed to identify problems early, when they are most easily treatable.

For all this headway, however, there are dramatic differences between plans, differences that are measurable and can shape your thinking about which to join. Many plans advertise free mammography and pap tests, for example, but the actual numbers of women who avail themselves of these services vary dramatically from plan to plan. This can be a clear indication about which plans are most serious about maintaining your good health by encouraging their doctors—and sometimes rewarding them materially—to make sure that these early-warning tests are conducted.

The National Committee for Quality Assurance last year measured more than three hundred plans with 65 percent of the nation's managed care plan members. (Many of the Committee's findings are reprinted in the appendix.) On average, 70 percent of the plans' women members who were 35 or older and had been with the plan at least a year had received a breast cancer screening in the past year—a good rate, particularly considering the reticence of some women to be tested, but one that fluctuated from plan to plan. At Group Health Northwest in Seattle, the rate nearly reached 90 percent and in thirty-one other plans from California to Kansas to Maine, the rate topped 80 percent. But in fifteen other plans, nearly half of them run by the large Cigna company, the recorded rate was below 60 percent. At Exclusive Health Care of Dallas, it was a mere 35 percent. Plans with low rates have maintained that in fact their performance is much better, but problems with data collection or computer system gaps caused artificially poor results. Cigna, for example, sharply disputes that the figures accurately reflect its performance, citing several factors it said held down the tallied results of some of its plans. The NCQA, however, stands by the importance of the results, even if they have been colored by poor data collection on the part of the plans. The committee's opinion is that problems with information gathering are themselves critical impediments to the monitoring that plans need to measure and improve their delivery of important services.

Rates for cervical cancer screening ranged from an almost perfect 98.3 percent at MDNY Health Care of New York to only 24.2 percent at Gulf South Health Plans based in New Orleans. Even in the same location, the rates can be substantially different. In New York, for instance, where MDNY scored so well, NYLCare did not. Its members were less than half as likely to have been tested, according to the results. Only 41.1 percent of their women members were recorded as having received a pap exam within the year. Cigna members were tested in less than 59 percent of the cases.

Testing is not the only area with wide disparities. The very style of medical treatment you receive—even during life's serious medical episodes—can be remarkably different depending on which plan you belong to. Let's look at three areas studied by the NCQA; average length of hospital stay for childbirth, the frequency of Cesarean section deliveries, and the frequency of hysterectomies.

Average Length of Hospital Stay

Drive-through deliveries may have become the biggest focus of rage during the managed care revolution, but not all plans press women to leave the hospital as quickly. For all plans measured by the NCQA, the average hospital birth stay was a little more than two days. Yet, the Aetna USHC plan in Delaware averaged nearly four days a stay. On the other side of the ledger, the Avmed plan that operates across Florida averaged below two days a stay in five of its six offices. Thirteen of the thirty-seven Cigna plans measured across the country had average stays of less than two days. One Virginia Mason plan had an average stay of 1.3 days. Because a few complicated deliveries can bring up the average of a modest-sized health plan, even an average length of stay of two days indicates that many women and babies are checked out in less time.

In an environment where health plans make money by getting you released from the hospital quickly, this information can be telling. But for you to form a fair opinion of a plan, it has to be used in conjunction with other data. Remember that for many women, getting out of the hospital quickly is the goal. For them, convalescing at home is vastly preferable to staying at the hospital. And many a plan with low average stays will argue that this is a reflection of good management rather than a move 'em out policy.

Cesarean Delivery Rate

In the past several years, medical researchers have criticized the numbers of Cesarean section deliveries in the United States as compared with other Western countries. The procedure has come to be seen as vastly overused—a fast, high-tech procedure that can speed delivery but only at a cost of needless trauma for the mother. On top of this, the procedure is far more expensive than natural childbirth, particularly when the mother's longer recovery period is considered. Thus, a well-managed plan can save itself money while providing what in most cases is a preferred manner of care.

On average, one in five babies is delivered by Cesarean section around the country, but, again, the performance of health plans differs widely. The Prudential plan in Cincinnati and the First Priority HMO of Northeast Pennsylvania each had Cesarean rates of under 10 percent. Twenty-four other managed care plans measured by NCQA had rates of under 15 percent, three of them affiliates of Prudential of Ohio. But eight of the plans had rates of more than 30 percent, three of them Prudential plans in South Florida and Arizona. The highest proportion of Cesareans was found at Blue Cross and Blue Shield of Western New York, where 38.4 percent of the births—far more than one in three compared to the national average of one in five—came through Cesarean section. Here, one can attribute differences to regional variation only so far. Rates for plans in the same region often differed by 10 percentage points or more. And since bringing down the numbers of costly Cesareans should be in the economic self-interest of health plans, high Cesarean rates may be an indication of management difficulties. If you are thinking of having a baby, you should consider which plan appears to have a strong commitment to holding down needless Cesareans.

Hysterectomy Rate

The number of hysterectomies per thousand women between the ages of forty-five and sixty-four is another telling figure that differs greatly among plans. The national average is just over nine and many researchers suspect that this number is needlessly high. Many plans have rates of twelve or more. Some, like CIGNA in San Diego, Foundation Health of California, Harvard Community Health, and Health New England, have rates of under six. The large Health Insurance Plan, or HIP, in New York has a rate of one. Two Prudential plans—in Pennsylvania and South Florida—have rates below one, and another Prudential plan, in Corpus Christi, Texas, did not authorize a single hysterectomy during the measured year.

How much weight to put on this information is a decision each woman has to make for herself. Many, for example, may well be drawn to plans with low hysterectomy rates. But for Marianne Lynch of Sacramento the issue was trying to get her plan to *approve* a hysterectomy that it had denied. She suffered from a rare type of fibroid so painful that it caused psychological as well as physical grief. Her gynecologist cautioned her that even if the fibroid was removed there was a strong chance it would grow back. "I was in therapy because this was so emotionally destructive to me," she recalled. "I was thirty-eight. I never had children and had absolutely no desire to have children. When I discussed the whole situation with my gynecologist, he agreed that for me a hysterectomy would probably be the best solution." Her request was originally denied by her health plan, but Marianne prevailed on an appeal to a medical panel assembled by the plan. Last May 25, Marianne had her operation.

Marianne's story is an example of how individual medical priorities and needs are. But regardless of a woman's partic-

WOMEN'S ISSUES

ular preferences, there are steps that you can follow to ensure you have the best chance of getting the coverage you want. At the very least draw up a mental list of the medical issues most important to you and then amass the information you need to make sure they are addressed.

[1] *As suggested in advice about choosing any doctor, if you prefer women doctors, call the ones near you listed in the plan directory and see if they have appointments available*. Before choosing, ask to meet them to determine whether their medical approaches and personalities are to your liking. If they don't have time to sit down with you, they probably shouldn't be your doctor.

[2] *If you are concerned about maintaining your health rather than only seeing your doctor when you are sick, find out what free tests the plan offers—and check to see how often members make use of them.* You can do this by checking the appendix and asking an individual plan for information not listed. If a low proportion of members avail themselves of the tests, you probably have an indication that the plan is not going to aggressively monitor for cancer and other illnesses. If the plan says it cannot furnish a figure for the percentage of women members who regularly receive pap tests or mammograms, it is as telling as a low rate.

[3] *If you are considering getting pregnant, try to determine whether your plan is likely to help you go through the birthing process in the manner you choose.* If you have a satisfactory relationship with your ob-gyn, is this doc-

tor on the plan's panel? If you will use a doctor and hospital outside the plan's panel, find out the plan's reasonable and customary allotment for the pregnancy, then check it against your doctor's and hospital's charges. For example, if the plan pays 80 percent of the cost of a pregnancy for charges up to $5,000 and your doctor and hospital charge a total of $8,000, your out of pocket expense would be far higher than the 20 percent co-payment you might have expected to pay. The plan will pay $4,000—80 percent of the $5,000 ceiling it set—and you will pay the other $4,000. This is the total of the $3,000 difference between the $5,000 ceiling and the $8,000 bill and the $1,000 you owed as the 20 percent co-payment on the $5,000. If the plan had covered 80 percent of the full bill, your out of pocket cost would have only been $1,600.

If you prefer a midwife to deliver your baby rather than a doctor, does the plan allow this? Visit hospitals in your area to see their birthing rooms and maternity wards. The differences in setting can be pronounced. If you find a hospital to your liking, find out if it is affiliated with the plan. On your checklist, you might also want to find out how often the plan recommends scheduling prenatal appointments, whether it covers birthing classes and after-birth services, and under what conditions it recommends the use of epidurals and other drugs and Cesarean sections.

[4] *If you would like to be pregnant but are having trouble conceiving, it is important to read the plan's fine print.*

Many plans will pay for low-cost tests, but not for the high-tech costly treatments that doctors sometimes recommend to induce pregnancy. It is the rare plan that will pay for artificial insemination or egg implantation.

[5] *If you are an older woman, it is particularly important for you to find a plan that offers comprehensive cancer treatment.* The rates of breast and cervical cancer rise sharply once women reach their fifties, and they become even more pronounced in later years. How concertedly a plan monitors its members, through mammograms and pap tests, should be crucial to you. If a plan has high rates of hysterectomies and mastectomies, you have every right to question whether it is doing all it can to detect cancers before they spread.

| 6 |

THE BEST INSURANCE FOR YOUR CHANGING FAMILY

It might have been the most prosaic aspect of their union, but when Bill Johnson and Mary Collins married in 1996, they set themselves on a course of making insurance decisions that have already affected their medical care and pocketbook and will continue as the family they hope to build takes shape. The decisions started just a short while after their wedding and involved considerations about whether each of them would continue to carry their individual coverage or both join under one of their plans. Hundreds of dollars a year and questions of what risks they wanted to take as a couple weighed heavily. When children enter the picture, there will be a new round of choices that involve not only dollars and cents but the quality of care their children grow up with.

SINGLE VS. DUAL COVERAGE

When couples marry, it may seem that by definition their health insurance position improves. If both spouses are working at jobs with health coverage, they can continue to carry their own insurance. The advantages can be considerable: Some plans still carry the once routine benefit of picking up the co-payment charges left uncovered by the other plan. And in an era when many people lose or change jobs frequently, carrying two policies helps ensure that you will continue to have insurance coverage no matter what the twists and turns of your career.

For those like Bill and Mary, who are willing to give up one of their plans, there are advantages as well (see chart). In place of two monthly premiums there is one. Bill's monthly premium as a single person came roughly to twenty-six dollars a month. Because her employer covered a smaller proportion of the total premium cost, Mary's monthly out of pocket expense came to about forty dollars for roughly the same coverage. By receiving all their coverage through Bill's plan, the couple pays a total of about fifty-five dollars a month, or ten dollars less than they did for separate individual coverage. The saving comes to $120 a year, but it doesn't stop there. Mary's employer, like many other large companies, offers cash rebates to employees who decline to exercise their health insurance option sometimes as much as $1,000 a year.

THE CONSUMER'S GUIDE TO HEALTH CARE PLANS

In Mary's case, it came to $200. So the couple now saves more than $300 a year by combining coverage. "Getting coverage through Bill works out well in a lot of different ways," Mary said, pointing to some benefits, like free annual checkups, which she hadn't received before.

ONE PREMIUM MAY BE BETTER THAN TWO			
Bill's monthly premium	25.84	X 12	310.08
Mary's monthly premium	41.86	X 12	502.32
Joint premium	55.61	X 12	667.72

If the course of action for young couples seems cut-and-dried, rest assured that it is not. Many choices are barely understood by most people. And different choices will work for different couples. What *doesn't* work is the situation for all too many couples. It is clear that many families wind up paying far more for insurance and in return receiving coverage not nearly as comprehensive as they could secure. Newlyweds who continue paying premiums on two policies may needlessly be paying out hundreds of dollars more a year in extra premiums for redundant coverage. The parent who simply adds a newborn to his or her policy may wind up passing over plans with far more developed provisions for children and paying for such services as well baby visits and vaccinations that other plans provide without cost. Complicating your decisions are changes in law and insurance options, which make the certitudes of yesterday anything but givens today.

Consider the issues facing newlyweds. As stated, double

THE BEST INSURANCE

coverage presents certain benefits that may be worth the cost. Different plans may provide different covered services. One plan might feature solid management systems for illnesses like asthma that one spouse can benefit from. The other might include greater coverage of fertility treatments or other services of particular interest. The significance may be waning, however, for another already mentioned benefit that for many people has historically been worth the price: If either partner loses a job, coverage can easily be continued under the second policy.

The value of this benefit has been lessened by Federal legislation—the Kennedy-Kassebaum bill, which allows employees to automatically qualify for insurance, without medical exams or restrictions on preexisting conditions, when they switch jobs. But the importance of this legislation can be overemphasized. Under COBRA legislation, employees can keep their coverage for an extended period after leaving or losing a job by continuing to make monthly premiums. And because many employees who lose jobs wind up on unemployment for long periods or hook on with employers who don't offer insurance, the effect of this legislation has been less significant than many had expected.

The benefits of carrying two plans have otherwise been greatly altered over the years. It used to be that employers fully picked up the cost of dependents that a worker added to his or her coverage. Not anymore. Employees these days often pay from 20 to 40 percent of the cost for their own coverage through monthly premiums. But it is usually the case that they pick up a greater percentage of premium cost for their families. More and more, companies step down the proportion of premium cost they absorb, covering a higher proportion for their employees; a lower rate for a single dependent and a rate that is still lower for three or more dependents. For employees, this means that quite often they have to shoulder the entire premium themselves for the third person on their plan. This provides an incentive in many cases for both parents to maintain separate policies in instances when they are covered by separate employer-provided insurance. The employers will pick up a higher percentage of the cost for each parent. In addition, a company will often pay a higher rate for a child as a second dependent than it would if the child was a third dependent on the plan.

There is another incentive to maintain separate policies, particularly if neither is a pure HMO without deductibles and only token co-payments. It used to be that a family covered through two plans could have its entire medical bill picked up between the dual policies. If the first paid a full bill minus a 20 percent co-payment, the other plan would typically pick up the co-payment.

Today, this is less often the case. Now, if one plan offers a somewhat better payment rate than the other, it will usually only make up the difference between the rate of the first plan and the rate it pays. This is how it works: An employee is on her own point-of-service plan, which has a 30 percent co-payment. She is also carried on her husband's fee-for-service policy, which has a 20 percent co-payment. She receives a $100 medical bill and pays thirty dollars of it herself. A few years ago, her husband's plan probably would have covered the thirty dollars, but not anymore. Nowadays, it will likely pick up ten dollars of her co-payment—the difference between what its 20 percent co-payment would have covered and what her less favorable plan picked up. Over the course of a year, this difference between old reimbursement methods and new ones can cost hundreds of dollars.

INFERTILITY, PREGNANCY, AND CHILDREN

If you are willing to carefully plot out your medical costs, there is one undeniable plus to coverage through a single plan, the basic advantage Bill and Mary discovered: It can save an enormous amount of money. The cost of two premiums, meeting two deductibles, and if you are in a fee-for-service or point-of-service plan, paying co-payments, can be needlessly expensive.

Once you settle on your strategy for coverage as a couple, your next big deliberations are likely to come when you decide to have children. For couples who have trouble conceiving, the differences among plans in coverage for fertility services will probably become starkly apparent. There are widely varying degrees of coverage for counseling, laboratory and genetic testing, and routine examinations. Many plans will cover voluntary sterilization and abortion. Almost all will cover some tests for infertility. Few, if any, will cover the most high-tech fertilization procedures, which can easily cost more than $10,000, although in some states plans are mandated by law to cover in vitro fertilization. There are variations, usually over the number and kinds of tests that plans will authorize.

If your coverage contract seems hard to understand, get more information from plan representatives, backed up by letters explaining specifically what services are covered.

Issues of maternity coverage were covered in the previous chapter. Don't take it as a given that the plan with the best pregnancy coverage also has the best coverage for children, or that if you are satisfied with your plan, it will be good for your children, too. For couples with newborns, it is effortless and seemingly natural to simply add your baby to your coverage. But, if you would like to use a particular pediatrician and this doctor is not affiliated with your plan, the plan might suddenly be the wrong one for you. And setting aside for the moment the different services for children that various plans offer, there are financial considerations that can easily slip by when making your coverage decision. If each spouse is covered under a separate policy, you should make some quick computations about which is more worthwhile for your child. How much does each charge to carry an extra dependent? If you already have another child covered by one of the plans, will your rates increase more dramatically if you add your newborn to the same plan or turn for coverage to the other plan?

Beyond this, there are, of course, substantive issues of medical benefits and quality. If yours is a family covered by two plans, the choice between the two can affect not only your selection of doctors, but other important factors such as whether you have access to free classes for new parents and a twenty-four-hour-a-day medical hot line. Perhaps even more importantly, the plans with track records of concern for their members commit themselves to preventive services, like free well baby visits and concerted efforts to make sure children receive innoculations in a timely manner.

It is services like these that have earned the Group Health Cooperative of Puget Sound a strong reputation in the Seattle area. When Lynn Livesley moved back to the area a few years ago with her husband and newborn daughter, it was that reputation that drew her to the Group Health Cooperative plan. Well baby visits and innoculations are free to plan members. "We take advantage any time a patient is in to get him immunized, whether he is there for a formal well baby visit or not," said Dr. John Taylor, a pediatrician who, like all the Cooperative's doctors, is an employee of the plan. A database flags children who have fallen behind on their immunizations, and their parents are called for appointments. The results are apparent in statistics amassed by the NCQA, the main accreditation agency for managed care plans. Nationally last year, 65.3 percent of the children who were members of individual plans for a least a year were current on their immunizations. At Puget Sound, the figure was 89.1 percent, one of the highest rates in the country. For those who think one plan is more or less the same as another, the variation in rates offers contradictory information. Rates ranged from 93.9 percent for the Cigna plan in Oklahoma to 20.9 percent for the Cigna plan in St. Louis. As mentioned earlier, Cigna, as well as other plans, disputes the accuracy of some low scores, but the NCQA believes that they are important measures—either of a plan's performance or its difficulty in accurately measuring its performance. This, the committee believes, can seriously impede efforts to improve. (A complete listing can be found in appendix A.)

Other measures of a plan's effectiveness in addressing and treating children's health needs are also significant and should be investigated by parents who are considering a number of plans. Checkups are, of course, essential for babies, but they are also necessary for children of every age. Again, the variation among plans is extreme, with the NCQA recording an annual well child visit rate for teenagers of under 5 percent for some plans and more than 70 percent in one case—that of a sister plan to Puget Sound in Wisconsin, Group Health Cooperative of Eau Claire.

PEDIATRIC CHRONIC CONDITIONS

Although it is the last thing parents want to think about, millions of children develop chronic conditions that should receive attention that goes beyond the basic complement of checkups, innoculations, and treatments for occasional ear aches and colds. One analysis of data indicates that about 20 million children under eighteen, or about 31 percent of the juvenile population, have one or more chronic health conditions, excluding learning disabilities and mental health conditions. Yet, critics of managed care say the kinds of varied, coordinated services that should be the foundation of treatment for most of these conditions is often lacking.

If, as your child grows, it emerges that he or she has any chronic problems, asthma being the most prevalent, look for a plan that has developed a meaningful case management program for the illness. Along with qualified specialists, the plans most committed to truly managing these illnesses offer a host of other services. These include home visits, to make sure environment and diet are not contributing to symptoms, patient education on administering drugs and using medical devices, and professional patient liaisons, whose job it is to coordinate treatment among primary care doctors and various specialists and other medical professionals, like therapists. Many plans say they offer such coordination, but critics argue that too often the contentions are more hype than fact.

How to distinguish fact from marketing fabulation? First, look for hard, documented results. Some of the most measurable results involve asthma, by far the most prevalent chronic ailment among children and the one most responsive to effective, coordinated treatment. If pediatric asthma is not treated in a preventive manner, involving diet, cleansing the home of environmental irritants, and medication, a child can expect to make frequent trips to hospital emergency rooms for treatment of sudden, often frightening outbreaks. If the child learns how to monitor symptoms, if effective drugs are prescribed on a schedule that can work around school schedules, and if his family keeps an environment free of dust and other contaminants, the chances are he will never have to race to an emergency room at all. Ask any plan you are considering what percentage of its children have visited emergency rooms because of asthmatic conditions.

Next, ask the plan how long its disease management program has been in operation and how proactive it is. Because asthma is so prevalent and so responsive to cost-effective treatment, many plans are trying to develop comprehensive programs. Match them against that of the Harvard-Pilgrim plan in Massachusetts, which has evolved over a decade. It has reduced emergency room and hospital visits by roughly 80 percent. Under the Harvard plan, according to Dr. Dirk K. Greineder, who was instrumental in developing the program, all pediatricians are required to attend four classes to help them recognize subtle symptoms of the disease and respond to them effectively. A central team made up of an allergist, a child mental health expert, and three nurses visits the plan's twenty-four clinics providing advice to doctors, teaching children how to use inhalers, talking to family members about dust control at home and cutting down on smoking, and reviewing the most complicated cases, sometimes by doing intensive examinations of the children themselves. And if any child winds up in a hospital emergency room because of asthma, team members step in to review the case, sometimes going so far as to make home visits. This goes much further, obviously, than the plan whose asthma program involves little more than instruction for doctors on how to teach children to use inhalers. For the family where both spouses maintain individual health coverage, the distinction should not be lost when deciding which one to enroll your child with.

As managed care plans mature and evolve, it makes sense for you to revisit your decision at least every couple of years to investigate whether yesterday's lagging plan has developed a state-of-the-art disease management system. As the years move on, too, keep one other part of the fine print in your plan contract in mind. When your children are ready to go off to college, check to see whether the plan covers dependents who live outside its normal service area. If it does

THE BEST INSURANCE

not, you will likely have to spend several hundred dollars a year on an additional policy offered through a college.

In summary, keep these points in mind:

[1] *If you are newly married, take the time to add up whether it will be wiser for the two of you to be under one plan or to maintain your individual coverage.* Look most specifically at cost. Add up the premium, the money you would receive from your employer in return for forgoing coverage, and the difference of two deductibles versus one family deductible. But also weigh unquantifiable factors, such as how comfortable you would be carrying one plan in a job market that frequently turns uncertain.

[2] *Beware of carrying too much coverage.* There used to be real monetary advantages to double coverage, but these have shrunk somewhat over the years because of protections afforded by COBRA regulations and other Federal laws. As a result, the mental security that carrying two plans may give you very often is not matched when weighed against the dollar savings provided by single-plan coverage.

[3] *If you have a new child, do a dollars-and-cents analysis of your alternatives.* If you are covered by two plans, work out which employer will cover more of the premium cost for your new child, which plan provides basics like

immunizations and well baby visits free of charge, and which has lower deductibles and co-payments.

[4] *Also perform a medical analysis.* Check which plan includes a favored pediatrician or hospital. And measure the plans' records on making sure children receive regular checkups and timely innoculations.

[5] *If your child suffers from a chronic illness, investigate whether your plan has special programs to deal with it.* These should involve coordinated services, easy access to specialists, and education on disease management.

| 7 |

THE NEW WORLD OF MEDICARE

The enactment of the Medicare program in 1965 was a remarkable boon to senior citizens. But Ralph Thompson of West Covina, California, and millions of other older Americans believe they have found something even better for their medical needs. Like thousands of older Americans decide every week, Ralph chose to forsake the traditional Medicare program and join a Medicare HMO. There was a downside: Because his doctors and hospital were unaffiliated with the plan he chose, Kaiser Permanente of Southern California, he had to give them up—and they had been integral to his life for twelve years, successfully treating him for cancer of the larynx and monitoring his health and medications. "It was difficult," he said. "It was difficult, believe me."

But Mr. Thompson, a retired salesman, soon found that the benefits easily outweighed the difficulty of the transition. He turned out to be just as satisfied with his new medical team. And he accomplished what he set out to do in making the change: cutting his health expenses by hundreds of dollars a year.

When he was covered by the traditional Medicare program, Mr. Thompson paid monthly premiums that in 1998 came to $43.80 and received reimbursement for 80 percent of his doctor bills after the first $100 spent annually and the full cost of sixty days of hospital care minus a $760 deductible. He also received other assorted benefits that paid some portion of additional hospital costs and part of the bill for such services as home health care, laboratory work, outpatient hospital services, and skilled nursing home care. Often, though, the proportion of costs covered still leaves Medicare recipients with substantial bills. Medicare coverage of hospital bills drops dramatically for beneficiaries who spend more than sixty days as patients. For days sixty-one through ninety the patient has to cover $190 each day out of pocket. And things get worse from there.

So, like fully one-third of the 38 million Medicare recipients, Mr. Thompson added to this basic coverage by also taking out a supplementary policy known as Medigap insurance. This policy reimbursed Mr. Thompson for the deductibes and co-insurance payments that Medicare did not cover.

But over the years, the cost of the Medigap coverage

THE NEW WORLD OF MEDICARE

began to mount—from the forty-eight dollars a month he paid in the mid '80s to the $133 a month he was paying in 1997, when he decided to make a change. Only adding to his sense of financial pressure was the fact that other Medigap policies, which covered such valuable benefits as drugs and eyecare, were simply beyond his means.

Medicare HMOs are particularly plentiful in Southern California, where Mr. Thompson lives, and the benefits they offer in this region, for complicated reasons relating to Medicare procedure, are particularly generous. As he investigated plan after plan, he found startling financial advantages in any number of them. In choosing Kaiser, Mr. Thompson found a good deal of savings. He continues to pay his basic Medicare premium, most of which is assigned to Kaiser. He has to use doctors and hospitals affiliated with the plan. But when he uses a doctor, his co-payment is only three dollars. One hundred days of hospital care are completely covered, and after a sixty day wait, Mr. Thompson is eligible for another one hundred days of coverage. He is also eligible for free lenses and sixty dollars toward the purchase of a pair of eyeglass frames every two years. And he can now obtain three drugs that were costing him $840 a year out-of-pocket in one hundred day doses for co-payments of only seven dollars each.

"It has been one of the best things I've ever done," he said.

Mr. Thompson is one of the five million senior citizens who have abandoned the traditional Medicare program in the last decade to join HMOs specifically designed to attract them. More than 13 percent of the 38 million Medicare beneficiaries have left the regular plan for the HMOs, which are beginning to sprout up widely across the country. In many ways, this migration is the most sweeping change to affect Medicare since its inception in 1965.

The traditional Medicare program has always offered substantial coverage for many major medical services in exchange for the 20 percent co-payments and relatively modest monthly premiums to help cover hospital costs. It has been a one-size-fits-all program in which every recipient, young or old, healthy or sick, wealthy or not, has been subjected to the same charges and made eligible for the same services. With monetary pressures on the program preventing it from expanding covered services, significant medical needs—like the drug and eyeglass costs that meant so much to Mr. Thompson—have never been covered through Medicare, opening the way for the ten versions of Medigap, the private, supplemental insurance policies authorized by the Federal government that cover different combinations of additional benefits.

Now, through Medicare HMOs and other variations, the Federal government is encouraging radical shifts in the Medicare program. The uniformity of coverage is being replaced with consumer choice and a collection of options that is only growing. For one thing, new regulations will make it far easier for the plans to spread in rural, low-cost medical areas.

Other options are also being made available through legislation. At least some older Americans now have the option to open what are called medical savings accounts in which they can invest the money that would have gone toward Medicare premiums and use it for health care expenses. A limited number of others will soon be able to strike deals in which they can pay doctors far more than the prescribed Medicare rates for treatment, thereby insuring care from doctors who might otherwise turn them away. And, as a result of soon to be implemented rules, almost every Medicare recipient is about to be deluged with promotional material from Medicare HMOs new and old, ones run by insurers and ones run by doctors and hospitals, that promise the world in exchange for a signature on a dotted line. Even without the new regulations, the pressure for Medicare recipients, particularly those who are financially hard pressed, to abandon the traditional program is growing independently—for one thing, Medicare premiums are expected to double in the next ten years.

If the new opportunities sound like win-win situations, rest assured that they aren't. The impact of the HMOs, in particular, on senior citizens and on the Medicare program itself can be far more varied than the happy experience of Mr. Thompson. Each alternative presents its own complications, which are frequently difficult for senior citizens to grasp, particularly when bombarded with rose-colored promotional material from a host of plans. If not extremely careful, Medicare recipients can find themselves shut off from doctors and drugs they have come to rely on. And they can find their requests for such resources as skilled nursing facilities being scrutinized far more carefully.

Although in the immediate future the broader implications may mean little to older Americans, there is also a great public policy debate underway about whether Medicare HMOs will wind up draining money from the traditional Medicare program and threatening the care of the oldest and sickest Americans, who are most likely to remain in the Government plan. The fear is that the HMOs will actively work to attract the customers they want most—the young and the healthy—leaving the patients who would be less profitable to them in the traditional program. The existing Medicare program would no longer have the surpluses created by the premiums of healthier recipients to cover the cost of care for the more sickly. The results could be grim—fast rising premiums for people who are usually in the worst position to afford them, as well as deteriorating medical care. A financially ailing Medicare system would be in no position to maintain its reimbursement levels for doctors and many of the most talented ones could opt to drop out of the program.

Whatever the effects, the opportunity offered by the HMOs can still be overwhelmingly attractive, particularly for younger, robust seniors. But not for everyone. In exchange for far better coverage for the dollar, plan members must agree to the restrictions that define all HMO plans. Patients must use the doctors and hospitals affiliated with their plans. For the elderly, this can be a crushing restriction. Sometimes it means ending a relationship with a doctor that in retrospect can seem irreplaceable. Sometimes a patient with a chronic, complicated condition may have to break up a team of specialists he or she has assembled to minister to a tricky, idiosyncratic condition.

BOXED IN BY AN HMO

Perhaps most wrenching of all are cases where a patient contracts an illness that can best be treated by a specialist or hospital outside the plan's panel. In most of these situations, the plan member has little recourse. He or she can appeal to the plan for permission to see the doctor, but these dispensations are rare. Plans typically find affiliated doctors who have the credentials to perform the same procedures on which the outside experts have built their reputations. Factors such as whether the plans' doctors have as much experience or whether they could do it as well are usually not taken into serious consideration. Similarly, when members petition plans to pay for unorthodox treatments that are often a last recourse, the plans typically reject such requests, labeling the treatments experimental or unnecessary.

The problems of being tied exclusively to a health plan's affiliated providers hit home to George Thomas, a retired navy fighter pilot from San Diego. Three years ago, Mr. Thomas, now seventy-four, developed an aching pain in his neck that led him to visit his doctor, who was affiliated with his Medicare HMO, FHP International. The doctor sent him to one of the plan's orthopedic specialists, but his problems persisted, according to Mr. Thomas's son-in-law, Christopher Cain. The doctors prescribed painkillers and the pain subsided, but soon Mr. Thomas was experiencing a loss of energy, an extreme drop in weight, and all-around discomfort. His doctors responded by sending him to an FHP-affiliated hospital and a special nursing facility linked to it. But, for all this, when Mr. Cain came back from a lengthy business trip, he recalls, "I saw him and I said, 'This man's dying.'"

His father-in-law, who used to weigh more than 160 pounds, was now an emaciated 114. Mr. Cain turned to his personal physician for advice. The doctor told him to try to reach the plan's medical director. A spokesperson for PacifiCare, the company that has since taken over FHP, says there is no record of Mr. Cain or anyone else from Mr. Thomas's family trying to contact the plan with their concerns. "We were not contacted about any questions or concerns about the care of Mr. Thomas," she said. But Mr. Cain said he placed at least eight calls to the company, being put on hold for fifteen or twenty minutes before finally reaching representatives who told him they didn't know the name of the medical director or who referred him back to Mr. Thomas's doctors. "We decided there was no time left," he said. "I don't think he had another week or two."

Mr. Cain called an ambulance and immediately sent Mr. Thomas to UCLA Medical Center in Los Angeles. UCLA was also affiliated with FHP, but it was outside Mr. Thomas's coverage area. The plan told the family that it would not reimburse the cost of Mr. Thomas's stay. This was at least in part because the plan had no indication before this that there were concerns about the care Mr. Thomas was receiving through his usual providers, the PacifiCare spokesperson said earlier this year. Mr. Cain maintained the plan was contacted numerous times. "One of the things that happens is they just blow you off," he retorted. "I'm sure they have no record."

In any event, here is where Mr. Thomas's grandson stepped in—Dean Cain, the actor who played Superman on the television show *Lois and Clark*. Dean put $30,000 on his credit card as a guarantee against the bills Mr. Thomas would incur. Eventually, the expenses mounted to $140,000 in a single month. But within a few hours of admission, doctors successfully traced Mr. Thomas's problem to an infection in the bones of his spine. Arduous treatment, experimental drug cocktails, and rehabilitation ensued. Mr. Thomas's health is vastly improved. And after his family filed a lawsuit against FHP, a check from the plan turned up in the mail covering the $140,000. Still, the family is continuing to press the suit, claiming pain, suffering, and a loss of health that Mr. Thomas will never fully reclaim. PacifiCare is arguing it was without legal merit.

Meanwhile, Medicare recipients would be wise to consider the larger lesson of Mr. Thomas's case—that without a wealthy family behind you, you will find it difficult to breakdown the restrictive walls of your HMO.

Two years ago in Queens, New York, Nadine Hemy experienced similar problems. After his retirement, her father, Elio, continued receiving health insurance from his longtime employer and additionally maintained a supplemental Medicare policy. But after attending a luncheon at a neighborhood diner sponsored by US Healthcare he decided to make a significant switch in his coverage. Representatives of the managed care plan laid out advantages of its Medicare HMO that seemed too good to pass up. Appealing to him most were free prescriptions and eyeglasses. His wife, Miriam, had faltering vision and he regularly took expensive drugs for a heart condition. He dropped his Medigap policy and signed up, thinking he had made an economically shrewd move.

But within a month, Miriam suffered a fall and sustained broken blood vessels in her brain. Although she was discharged from the hospital after three days with a clean bill of health, when she underwent a follow up CT-scan three weeks later, it turned out that her cranial cavity was filled with blood. An emergency craniotomy was performed at a local hospital and as Mrs. Hemy convalesced, social workers at the hospital recommended that her next stop be at a "traumatic brain injury treatment center." At the center, called Kingsbrook, Nadine's mother was to undergo intense therapy designed to engage her mind and get her brain functioning again. The next day, the social workers said they had changed their mind—that Kingsbrook would not have been a proper setting for her.

Nadine said that under her persistent questioning, "They had to admit to me it was the HMO who turned my mother down." This set the stage for a protracted battle between Nadine and the HMO, with her mother's hospital stay stretching on past two months without any recuperative therapy to speak of being performed. "I was at the end of all my alternatives, so I called Kingsbrook and cried to the person in charge of admissions," she recalled. " 'If she were me,' he said, 'I would take her off the HMO.' " Nadine did just that, and after another month's wait, Mrs. Hemy returned to conventional Medicare coverage. "When I disenrolled her and went back to straight Medicare, boom, like magic she's in Kingsbrook." There she began receiving the treatment her daughter had hoped to provide for her months earlier, when the chances of full recuperation were far greater. "The doctors told me if she went there when she should have, maybe the outcome wouldn't have been as grim," Nadine said. "It's been almost two years. Her brain has been damaged."

It is situations like these that have kept millions of Medicare recipients in the traditional program, where choice of doctors and hospitals is virtually limitless and where officials are very often more likely to approve medical recommendations made by doctors. Drugs are another element of care that can be greatly limited by the HMOs, which maintain their own formularies. In many cases similar drugs that are supposed to treat the same ailments behave differently in different people. To give up a particular brand drug that has worked for you over the years can be a major sacrifice. While Medicare does not cover drug costs, many Medigap policies do. When people join a Medicare HMO they usually forego buying a Medigap policy, which would seemingly be largely duplicative in coverage. The advantage of staying with the traditional Medicare arrangement is also more pronounced for older and sicker beneficiaries. It is these people who have more likely put together teams of doctors to treat complicated conditions and who have gained faith in physicians who have sometimes literally saved their lives. To say goodbye to this support is a price too high for many beneficiaries to pay.

THE CONSUMER'S GUIDE TO HEALTH CARE PLANS

The willingness to take on risk varies from person to person. For senior citizens whose finances are often as fragile as their health, the temptations to save money through Medicare HMOs can be great. Depending on medical usage, an HMO can save in the hundreds of dollars a year by paying for eyeglasses and drugs and obviating the need for Medigap policies with price tags that can rise into the four figures. Yet, these plans make the most sense for those with the least risk—younger, healthier recipients. They can also be a boon to those who find their doctors, hospitals, and medications covered under one of the plans. For others, particularly patients who have histories of chronic illness that have been treated well by their physicians, the best advice is often to stay put and try to find a Medigap policy that will complete the insurance package.

This in itself can be a challenging task. With Medicare HMOs signing up healthier recipients, Medigap rates have been soaring and plans frequently refuse applicants because of their medical histories. For many with serious ailments, the only options are a handful of Blue Cross plans and the policies offered through the American Association of Retired People, which accepts all comers, although their rates have close to doubled over the past few years. Almost all other plans screen out high-risk cases they see as potential money losers.

THE NEW WORLD OF MEDICARE

BEYOND HMOS

For all the uncertainties associated with HMOs, further experimentation with Medicare is only escalating. By next year, scores of hospitals and groups of doctors will be offering their own HMO plans, called *provider sponsored organizations* and they and the older plans will all be able to solicit seniors directly. At the same time, the great monetary advantages of these plans seem likely to shrink a bit. Plans have been finding it more difficult to turn a profit on the reimbursement rates allowed through the Medicare program. Rates to members have been rising in many cases and the breadth of services being offered is often shrinking.

Beyond the HMO model, Congress has authorized a few experiments over the past two years for limited numbers of Medicare recipients. Each has generated widespread controversy because of fear that they will weaken the already shaky finances of the Medicare program. But they may offer opportunities to older Americans, particularly wealthy ones.

The trial *Medical Savings Account* program allows people to use their Medicare premium money, more than $500 a year, in a novel way. A portion of it goes toward buying a high deductible insurance policy that leaves the account holder responsible for the first $2,500 in medical expenses. The remainder goes into a special account that can only be used for medical expenses. If the participant in this program remains healthy, the account accumulates interest-bearing funds that can be used for future medical expenses, making it effortless to meet the large deductible and also to cover co-payments and the cost of drugs.

The problem for account holders, of course, occurs before their account has grown, particularly if they are of limited means. They can count on paying as much as $2,500 a year for their medical costs, which are often unpredictable in life's later stages.

Sizable bank reserves minimize the discomfort. They also allow some older Americans to look with interest on another trial program. In this one, doctors are permitted to charge whatever the market will bear for treatments instead of what the fixed Medicare fee schedule calls for. In theory, the policy would allow the elderly to buy care that doctors do not offer to those prohibited from paying what they consider a fair price. But in order to participate in this program, doctors must agree not to see any Medicare patients for two years. Because so many of their practices are Medicare dependent, it is doubtful that many doctors will become involved in this program. But in affluent areas, you might find yourself with an opportunity to write your own ticket for care in a way that was unheard of before now.

Information about these programs and all Medicare options is available on the Internet at www.medicare.gov. Program officials are working to include, by late 1998, information about which plans and options are available by locality. For those who choose to investigate an HMO, it is important to ask several questions that hold the answers to what your coverage will provide and whether it meets your needs.

[1] *Ask yourself whether you are happy with your current doctors, hospitals, and medications and find out whether any Medicare HMO will cover all of them.* You can get this information by asking your doctors, reading the plans' published list of affiliated medical providers, and requesting a written copy of the company formulary from plan representatives. The depth of knowledge among the phone representatives of many plans can leave something to be desired. Don't join a plan on the basis of a verbal reassurance that it will cover your longtime drug. And be aware that formularies change. What is covered today can be replaced by another drug tomorrow.

Don't underestimate the effectiveness of a team of physicians you have put together over the years to treat your personal medical conditions. You might keep some of the members through an HMO, but to lose a part of your team simply may not be worth the dollar savings. And don't forget that it is routine for HMOs to require that a primary care physician authorize every visit to a specialist. If you use specialists frequently, this can be burdensome and frustrating.

[2] *Compare and contrast the details of hospital coverage and other features offered by different plans.* Issues that have been raised in previous chapters may be of particular concern to you. For example, it may be reassuring to find that a hospital you have come to trust is on a plan's panel, but how many days of care does the

plan cover at the hospital and is there any sort of co-payment? Is there an annual limit on the number of hospital days that are covered? A limit on the number of contiguous days? Does the plan limit its coverage of preexisting conditions—that is health conditions that have been diagnosed prior to a recipient joining the plan? How does the plan define and cover emergency room care at a hospital?

Many plans will not cover the cost of emergency room care if what a patient thought to be an emergency turns out to have been a false alarm. Other plans will cover the visit if the patient is deemed to have had a reasonable belief that emergency care was required. And how does the plan define "experimental treatments"? These are usually cutting-edge medical procedures that a patient's doctor may recommend in dire circumstances, but that a plan may deem so unproven and costly that they don't merit coverage.

The Medicare program itself has a complicated definition of what constitutes an experimental treatment ineligible for compensation. If a plan you are interested in has an even more restrictive definition, it is something for you to be aware of, particularly if your medical history is poor. If you have suffered from a recurring series of ailments of a particular kind—a certain form of cancer or a faulty heart—it is worth discussing with your doctor what kinds of procedures you may want to avail yourself of if your condition deteriorates. It is then important for you to obtain a written statement guaranteeing such a procedure can qualify for coverage from the prospective plan.

[3] *At this point, compare price.* Medicare HMOs can differ widely in cost. In some parts of the country, a few plans allow you to join for no extra cost. Others charge as little as ten or fifteen dollars a month. Small dollar differences per month, though, can add up to substantial ones over a year—the difference between a ten dollar a month premium payment and a thirty-five dollar payment is $300 a year. Co-payments, as relatively small as they are, also vary. The annual cost difference between a three dollar co-payment and a fifteen dollar one can easily rise into the low hundreds of dollars. Before he chose Kaiser, Mr. Thompson, the retired salesman, analyzed information from seven other plans as well. He found doctor co-payments ranging from zero to five dollars. Drug co-payments varied from five dollars for a thirty day supply to seven dollars for a one hundred day supply. Furthermore, some plans capped drug reimbursements at between $1,700 and $2,500 a year, while Kaiser had no limit.

[4] *Find out what extra services the plan includes—in other words, what the plan gives you for your money.* Among the services not covered in the standard Medicare program are drugs, eyeglasses, home care, and medical equipment. Almost every Medicare HMO covers some of these; few cover all of them. Make sure the plan you are considering covers the ones that you use most

frequently or, given your medical history, may use in the future.

Distinctions between plans are important. The circumstances under which home care is covered differ widely. Some plans cover it only after protracted hospital visits, while other plans, seeing home care as an alternative to costly hospitalizations, provide it in a wider variety of situations. The kinds of devices and medical products that a plan will cover should be enumerated in its informational literature.

[5] *Check to see what preventive services, such as annual checkups and mammograms, the plan offers and encourages members to use.* The percentage of members who receive mammograms or checkups fluctuates dramatically from plan to plan. If protecting your health, rather than only treating your illnesses, is important to you, match records of different plans and check which have the highest proportion of members who actually receive the preventive services that the plans advertise. (See the appendix for information that can help you.)

[6] *If you decide to stay with the traditional Medicare program and, like the great majority of recipients, receive additional supplemental coverage as well, scrutinize Medigap plans to make sure you are getting the best deal.* The cost of Medigap policies has been skyrocketing as younger and healthier recipients leave traditional Medicare for HMOs. The migration has left the Medigap plans with a disproportionate balance of medically

needy policyholders, causing the escalation in premiums. But within this upward spiral, the variance in cost from one plan to another offering identical coverage can be shocking—some cost double the amount of others.

Under a Federal law enacted in the early '90s, companies can offer only ten prescribed packages of covered services. Some combinations offer eyeglasses, for example, while others don't. Others provide more extensive hospital coverage. The packages uniformly are denoted by letters from A to J. Some insurance companies may reject more applicants than others because of their health histories, but when it comes to services covered in any of the packages, the only difference is price. When *Health Pages* magazine surveyed Medigap plans in St. Louis two years ago, the prices offered by some plans were double those from others for identical combinations of services. Here is a sample of what the magazine found: Among ten organizations offering Plan A—the cheapest of the ten standardized plans and the one of greatest appeal to those on extremely limited incomes—the annual premium for a sixty-five-year-old woman varied from $379 offered by Physicians Mutual to $639 from United American Health Care. Remember, these prices cover *exactly* the same benefits.

By the time a woman reached seventy-five, the disparities grew even more extreme; the Physicians Mutual policy still cost $379 annually, but the premium at United American rose to $775. This means that a United American member paid more than twice as much as a Physicians Mutual member for the exact same services. In the popular Plan F, which covers the basic benefits offered in Plan A plus additional hospital and doctor deductibles and skilled nursing home care, annual premiums for a sixty-five-year-old woman varied from $865 at Christian Fidelity Life to $1,260 at Standard Life & Accident. To pay these extra dollars is simply to throw money away.

[7] *In addition to your decision about health coverage, you should carefully scrutinize the question of long-term care coverage, the insurance that is supposed to help cover bills for nursing homes and other providers of continuous care.* Many older Americans finance their nursing home stays through the Medicaid program. But to do this, they have to have assets valued at $60,000 or less. To accomplish this, tens of thousands of older people have "spent down" their assets by gifting them out to children and other relatives over a period of years. But Medicaid measures a person's assets as they were three years prior to entering the home.

For those who feel they may need nursing home care before their three year period expires, or who have not spent down their assets at all, long-term care insurance may seem attractive. But caution should be taken. Long-term care coverage varies dramatically, in terms of both cost and in services covered. With all of

THE NEW WORLD OF MEDICARE

your other medical costs and worries, it is tempting to choose among the cheapest plans, but too often these provide benefits that scarcely help with the huge costs of care in nursing homes, skilled nursing facilities (which provide a greater degree of medical care than nursing homes), and assisted living units.

The average premium for good policies at age sixty-five, according to the American Association of Retired Persons, cost about $2,600. That cost rises to $8,500 if a policy is first purchased at age seventy-nine. Match this against the expense of long-term care. The average cost of a year in a nursing home is $38,000, but in some parts of the country it can rise to as high as $9,000 a month. Three two-hour visits a week from a home health aide will cost you $8,400 over the course of a year. According to the National Association of Insurance Commissioners, standard plans can offer benefits amounting to between $1,500 and $7,500 a month for nursing home coverage, often with a cap on the number of years covered and an initial period, usually of between twenty and one hundred days, when the beneficiary has to cover the full cost. So there is a real danger that you can sign, and pay, for a plan that will not begin to help you make use of a quality home a reality.

Start by finding out what the monthly cost of good care is in your area. Then match this against the benefit you would receive from various long-term care policies. The decision is then yours as to whether the support from the policy will make it possible for you to use a quality home or other services while not exhausting your savings and whether it is worth the price of the premium. Because of the complexity of these plans, it is a good idea to avoid signing up for any of them too quickly and to rely on friends, family, and senior care advisors for guidance.

[8] *Be on guard for any hint of discrimination if you are an older Medicare recipient or one with a history of medical problems.* If you choose to join a Medicare HMO, this is your right, regardless of your age or health. HMOs are famous for marketing themselves to the relatively young and healthy. Some of them have held informational seminars in settings where Medicare recipients have to walk up a flight of stairs, effectively shutting out those who cannot negotiate the steps. In blatant and subtle ways, they have asked prospective members about their health histories—a ploy that violates Medicare regulations. In their marketing, they will usually show younger seniors and offer such amenities as free exercise classes, which mean next to nothing to those dealing with more basic health needs.

Don't let the marketing dissuade you from a plan that otherwise meets your standards. Don't answer improper questions about your personal health history. Among the questions often asked by sales people that are out of bounds: how your general health is, whether you have ever had a heart attack or been treated for cancer or other illnesses, whether you are seeing a doctor now for specific problems, or even how old you are. Be sure to report such illegal inquiries to Medicare authorities (listed in the Federal pages of your phone book under Health Care Financing Administration) so that others don't experience the same discrimination.

| 8 |

FOR THE CHRONICALLY ILL

Joan Kitts is, in many ways, a believer in managed care. She feels that by structuring treatment more carefully, it can correct such abuses as needless regimens of care and paying duplicate fees for more or less the same service. And, she said, her own plan, MetraHealth, which she joined about two years ago in her hometown of Roanoke, Virginia, has saved her money. But she has also come to believe that the managed care principle "is wonderful unless you have, or are the parent of a child with, a chronic illness."

Mrs. Kitts's daughter, Amy, is a bright and determined sixteen-year-old high school junior. Since she was three years

FOR THE CHRONICALLY ILL

old, she has had diabetes but has hardly let this limit her activities. She is a black belt in karate and has received consistently impressive grades in school, running a 3.5 grade point index two years ago. Then, at the onset of puberty, the illness seemed to take an unpredicted turn. She gained twenty pounds in six weeks. She would leave school nauseated and her usually riveted focus gave way to extreme fatigue. Her grade point average fell to 2.6. Her blood sugar count soared, and her insulin need rose threefold. Amy's trusted primary care doctor was stymied. "He told me point blank he was stumped," Mrs. Kitts recalled. Both agreed there was something they weren't identifying. But by her account, it took her managed care plan close to a year to approve a referral to a specialist, a pediatric endocrinologist, who could help. There were none affiliated with the plan in Roanoke. She and Amy's primary doctor fought the plan's suggestion that she see an internal medicine doctor with a subspecialty in diabetes, but no pediatric background. Finally, the plan changed its mind and allowed a referral at its in-plan rate to a specialist at the University of Virginia, two and a half hours away.

"It took him about ten minutes to see that her thyroid was enlarging," Mrs. Kitts recalls. "He said it was a very, very common thing for female diabetics to have, but it typically happens when they are in their thirties or forties." The diagnosis was a major step in trying to restore Amy's health, but there were others, and it seemed that at each turn there was another battle.

First, MetraHealth would only pay for insulin packed and shipped from a regular supplier in Texas. Amy's doctor and her parents wanted her to use the fresher supplies from a local manufacturer. Eventually, the plan allowed this. Next, Mrs. Kitts had to fight for coverage of syringes and blood monitoring equipment. Then the battle turned to coverage for a nutritionist. Amy's endocrinologist believes this kind of help is essential for developing a new diet and training Amy in how to follow it. This, Mrs. Kitts said last year, was defined by the plan as an uncovered educational service rather than a medical one. "I just don't know which way to turn," she said. "If they don't help, we're just going to pay for it." Mrs. Kitts has not lost perspective on what managed care, as represented by her plan, can and cannot do well. Once the plan agreed to cover any of the disputed services, she says, it did so in a highly professional way. It packages syringes and blood monitoring equipment in a diabetic equipment kit every month, for example. "My biggest problem is just the amount of time and effort it takes to convince them that these things are necessary."

WHERE THEORY FALLS SHORT

In theory, managed care should be particularly suited to the treatment of diabetes and other chronic care conditions, like asthma and arthritis, that require extra levels of coordinated treatment and planning. But in large numbers of cases, plan members come up against the same frustrations experienced by Mrs. Kitts and Amy. What is often lacking is a deep understanding of the disease and a sophisticated treatment plan, staffed by experienced professionals, that could ultimately save the plan money. "Chronic diseases are costly, but they are particularly costly if they're not managed appropriately from the start—that's the potential problem with managed care," observed Dr. Doyt Conn, an Atlanta rheumatologist and senior vice president for medical affairs of the Arthritis Foundation. "The strategy for managed care organizations is directed toward acute care."

Meanwhile, he said, "there has been a change in understanding of chronic disease." If they responded to this change well, managed care companies could probably increase earnings while fulfilling the self-defined mandate: intensely managing the care of their members, in this case some of their sickest members. But while there are programs offered by a number of plans that speak to this aspiration, for the most part, in the eyes of experts who deal with the care of chronically ill patients, instances of meaningful case management are usually the exceptions.

For arthritis, for example, doctors at Stanford University developed a six-week course led by a nonphysician trainer in which people with the illness learn to understand the causes of their arthritis, the factors that trigger painful flair ups, and sources for help in times of need. One result is that they consult doctors about half as much as they previously had. Another is that by and large they experience less pain and have better feelings about themselves and their ability to cope in the world. Dr. Conn and the foundation are shopping this approach to managed care companies. As of now, he said, few have come close to offering this. "Giving the person with the chronic illness the tools to help themselves is just alien to the way medicine is packaged now in most managed care organizations," he said. "The thrust is to get them in, get them out as quickly as possible, maybe give them medication. They're not focused on patient education and self-management. They're focused on seeing four patients an hour."

PLANS WITH PLANS

In fact, there are notable exceptions—plans that have developed case management strategies for asthma, AIDS, and other chronic illnesses. These usually provide easier access to specialists and coordinated teams revolving around knowledgeable primary care doctors. Aside from specialists, these teams can include nurses who serve as patient representatives with their own case loads. They smooth over bureaucratic problems and make sure the doctors are all operating on the same page. The programs can also include educational efforts that sometimes involve seminars, libraries of useful materials, and newsletters with tips on care and information about treatment breakthroughs.

Other plans have eased access to specialists who often serve as primary care doctors for people with chronic illnesses. United Health Care of Minnesota permits direct access to specialists, obviating the need for referrals from primary care doctors. For a higher co-payment, Blue Shield of California does the same. These efforts, however, are standouts—apart from the norm. How you find them, how you track down the best doctors and hospital care for yourself, how you select a health plan that acts like it's on your

FOR THE CHRONICALLY ILL

side rather than as an obstacle to the care you and your doctor want—these are the challenges for people with chronic conditions.

In many states, the choices are limited in the extreme. Plans have the right to turn down people with previously diagnosed chronic illnesses, i.e., preexisting conditions. Other companies will accept applicants, but only with a proviso that they will not cover care relating to the condition for anywhere from six months to two years. Last year, thanks to the Kennedy-Kassebaum health care legislation, many people were rescued from this insurance bind. Broadly speaking, if a worker leaves a job that provided health coverage, he or she cannot be turned down for coverage by an insurance company for medical reasons.

But millions of others who are looking for insurance for the first time or otherwise fall outside the provisions of the bill are still faced with the likelihood of rejection. For them, there are pool insurance plans of last resort in twenty-six states, designed to cover those who could not find coverage in the marketplace. The problem is that their premiums are almost always extremely high, often beyond the reach of many of the people they are supposed to be helping and their benefits are often bare bones. Several states, New York, New Jersey, Massachusetts, and Washington being the largest, offer their residents a far better deal than this through what are known as "guarantee issue" laws. Under these, any plan that wants to sell individual or, often, small group insurance, must accept all applicants, regardless of health.

If you or someone in your family suffers a chronic condition, finding out which plan makes the most sense for you requires a combination of common sense research and an understanding of some of the intricacies of managed care that are less than obvious. On top of this, there is the sobering fact that you may not discover just how responsive a plan is until you call on it for help. It of course helps to see how many specialists a plan lists in your area of concern. But, as Peter D. Fox, a managed care consultant in Chevy Chase, Maryland, observed, "What you really want to know, you can't find out. Is the plan going to make it difficult for you to access the specialists?"

Still, there are steps you can take to add to the chances that access to specialists—and more—will be there for you.

[1] *Start with your primary care doctor—is your current doctor in the plan you are thinking about joining?* If not, can the doctor recommend another physician who is? Take the time to interview prospective primary care doctors before you join a plan. The doctor's knowledge of your illness and the ability of the two of you to communicate are, of course, important, but remember, too, that this doctor will be your prime advocate within the plan. If referrals to specialists or authorizations for medications or supplies are denied, this is the person in the best position to battle for your interests. Try to gauge whether this doctor is willing to represent you forcefully. Ask the doctor how the plan provides reimbursement—if it pays a capitated rate, does the doctor consider it adequate? Are there other plans he or she belongs to that pay more? This may affect how much

time the doctor is willing to devote to you and other plan members.

[2] *Review the plan's list of specialists and match them to your needs.* Many conditions require multiple specialists. Others, affecting children, are best treated by gastroenterologists, endocrinologists, and others who are juvenile specialists. Try to learn from primary care doctors how often the plan rejects referrals. Also, find out if the plan routinely allows multiple referrals—say four in half a year—to specific specialists needed by members with chronic conditions. Most beneficial, of course, are the rare plans that allow direct access to specialists without referrals or that allow specialists to act as primary care doctors.

[3] *Find out whether the plan has a case management system for your illness.* A carefully organized and staffed strategy can make all the difference between effective and compassionate treatment and haphazard coverage. Effective case management should include a core of knowledgeable primary care doctors, easy access to specialists, nurses or other trained professionals who act as patient advocates, timely listing of new treatment drugs on formularies, and the availability of the most specialized hospital care for your condition. Home visits to assess members' living environments can also be enormously helpful. Some plans, for example, have caseworkers visit the homes of asthma sufferers to see if there is anything in the air that triggers attacks or anything that can be placed in the home to

improve air quality. The best case management programs offer aggressive follow-up to hospitalizations, as well. A joint replacement, for example, would be followed by reimbursable physical therapy and a home visit in which a therapist makes sure devices are installed that make a patient's living environment easier to negotiate.

It would seem advantageous to plans to rely on case management approaches—to take the last example, a thoughtfully adapted home environment can reduce the chances of a fall that would lead to another costly hospitalization. Yet, most plans still do not offer case management for more than a handful—if any—of chronic illnesses. Dr. Conn, for example, said that, as of this writing, few had an effective case management plan for arthritis. The case management plans that can be found are priceless to patients. Asking a plan if it has one for your condition is a must, but it may only be the beginning of your investigation.

Within the industry, it is suspected that many plans that have developed reasonable management plans are less than eager to advertise them. If well publicized, these plans would be magnets for high-cost patients, leading the case management systems to work in a financially counterproductive way. One way to check further is to call local branches of any of the national associations that provide help to people with more than forty individual chronic conditions. The common knowledge of others with your condition can be invaluable.

FOR THE CHRONICALLY ILL

Also, press plans for more information than they usually dispense during enrollment drives. Prospective members frequently are barraged with a wide range of marketing brochures. These may minimize or avoid descriptions of the plans' case management systems for fear of attracting financially costly new members. Ask plans you are particularly interested in for more than these brochures. Ask as well for the welcome kits they give newly enrolled members. These kits are directed at a different audience—people whose care they must underwrite. It is in the plans' best interest at this point to describe and encourage the use of their case management programs.

[4] *Make sure the drugs you have come to rely on are listed on the plan's formulary.* Don't be satisfied if plan representatives tell you that in place of your drug the formulary lists generic substitutes that are identical. There have been numerous examples of patients who have found these drugs to be less satisfactory. Some plans have argued that the difference is purely psychological, but others point to differences in drug manufacture and packaging as factors that can produce lesser results. Also, check with your doctor to see how quickly after approval by the Federal Food and Drug Administration the formulary lists new, usually costly, cutting-edge drugs. Beyond the drugs themselves, ask or research what the plan covers in the way of supporting medical devices, items like Amy Kitts's syringe and blood monitoring equipment.

[5] *Check the precise description of how a plan determines if a treatment is considered experimental, and, therefore, outside the coverage limits of your agreement.* Typically plans will refuse to cover treatments not approved for coverage or deemed experimental by the Health Care Financing Administration, which runs the Medicare program. But significant differences between plans still remain, many of which are difficult to detect. For example, bone marrow transplants for certain conditions have been found to be effective, but for other conditions are still considered of unproven value and are therefore usually deemed experimental. Some sets of symptoms fall into gray areas that make it difficult, if not impossible, to assess whether they qualify for bone marrow coverage, particularly at a time when medical technology is expanding the chances of success with the procedure.

But there are ways to make a more informed assessment. Ask your doctor what cutting-edge treatments you might have to consider if your condition deteriorates. Then check with the local chapter of the chronic illness association that covers your condition—the American Heart Association, the Crohn's and Colitis Foundation, and the like—to see whether members have reported a pattern of coverage denials that can offer a guideline for you. And contact your state insurance department to ascertain whether there is a disproportionate number of complaints concerning coverage rejections for the plan you are considering,

FOR THE CHRONICALLY ILL

particularly for the procedures you may one day need to undertake.

[6] *Try to assess how easy it is to appeal denials of coverage.* For people with chronic illnesses, reliance is particularly high on unorthodox treatments, repeated referrals to specialists, special medical devices and paraphernalia, and tertiary specialists not affiliated with the plan. Denials of coverage can run high and members routinely have a right to appeal these rejections. But is the appeals process an open one? Does the plan offer you a case manager to help you formulate your case and put it before an appeals board? Do you have to appeal first to the very authorities who denied your request or is your appeal heard by a panel that had nothing to do with the decision? How many levels of appeal can you avail yourself of if your first challenge is rejected? It is the mark of a patient-centered plan if the process is extensively promoted, case managers are available to help members through it, and decisions are made by professionals who, if not quite independent, are at least not paid employees of the plan.

| 9 |

IF YOU HAVE
A MAJOR ILLNESS

Cancer. AIDS. Heart disease. The diagnosis of any of these illnesses—or many others with equally serious connotations—can be a crushing experience. But treatment breakthroughs have been remarkable. If caught early enough, the majority of cases are not life threatening anymore, provided up-to-date treatment is administered. Too often, however, the insurance system seems to pose impediments to getting this treatment rather than helping the patient. Many plans will refuse to insure people with previously diagnosed serious illnesses. Others will attach stipulations to coverage that preclude reimbursement for as long as two years for care they conclude is related to the diagnosed condition.

Still, for millions of people, HMO coverage can be a reality, available through employers, as a result of special legislation in some states, or from plans with liberal enrollment policies. Which plan can provide the best treatments available is the question for people with serious chronic illnesses, or those who because of heredity or lifestyle have a disposition toward them. As detailed in the last chapter, well-developed disease management plans are crucial. Access to cutting-edge treatments, procedures, and doctors can sometimes mean the difference between life and death. And in the normal course of treatment, the thoughtful coordination of services can mean the difference between feeling your plan is on your side and feeling that it is an enervating obstacle to your recovery.

THE FRUSTRATIONS OF A CANCER PATIENT

Audrey Storch of Wayne, New Jersey, was diagnosed with breast cancer in 1995 and underwent a successful lumpectomy, followed by chemotherapy. Her hospital stay went smoothly and her health has held up well. The very success of her core medical experience, however, underscores the difference between a plan that coordinates its treatment and one that doesn't. Audrey's did not. When her husband, Michael, went to the local pharmacy to fill three prescriptions ordered by her doctor, things seemed fine enough, but the plan later rejected reimbursement, according to Michael, claiming that the family had already reached its annual cap of $2,000 for drugs. As Audrey recovered, the family had to work out a credit with the pharmacy and obtain her drugs—at greater expense to the health plan—through the hospital.

When Audrey returned home after her hospital stay, she found one of her two young sons, now ages seven and nine, becoming uncharacteristically aggressive, obviously because of the tension kindled by his mother's illness. Audrey set out to get him counseling. "You need to pick a therapist you feel comfortable with," she said. "But we had to pick from a few therapists the plan selected." She rejected all of them and found her own therapist, who the family paid out-of-pocket until he affiliated with the plan, simply so that the family could receive reimbursement. "He had to fight for the number of visits he thought should be covered and the level of compensation he would receive," she said. To keep the therapy going, the analyst brought down his fee and the family paid for his continued services out of their own pocket.

During her recuperation, Audrey went for genetic testing to try to discover the root of her illness with, she said, the approval of a plan representative. But when the bill came due, it was denied. The plan said it had no record of the approval and that it ran counter to policy. Another fight ensued to win reimbursement. And when she began to suffer stomach problems as a result of her chemotherapy, she became enmeshed in still another argument with the plan. Her doctors prescribed one drug, but the plan would only allow reimbursement for another in the same chemical family. All in all, she is winning the battle against cancer, but, she reflected, "When you're fighting a life-threatening illness, the last thing you need to do is fight an insurance company. You're just too tired."

The best disease management programs provide the kind of coordination that Audrey's plan lacked. The fact that her doctors and hospital performed well underscores how important other factors are—nurses who could have made sure that the drugs she needed could be obtained without problem, specialists who could have counseled her on genetic testing, and ancillary practitioners, like therapists, who would have understood the counseling needs of families confronting serious illness. It has been pointed out that often this kind of coordination is more present in the breach than as the norm, even though, in theory it should be at the heart of good managed care. Yet, there are also many instances when plans, often acting in their own economic interests, but often in the interests of good health, develop systems that seem to fulfill the promise of the managed care concept. This can be true even in the costly treatment of AIDS.

A DECISION THAT WORKS

Of all the people requiring chronic, long-term care, no group requires treatment as sophisticated and rapidly changing as those with HIV or full-blown AIDS. Few if any deadly illnesses have so confounded modern researchers. At the same time, few, if any, have bent to a barrage of medical research as remarkably: What a couple of years ago was an illness that was inevitably fatal is now emerging as one that is manageable.

But the challenge of treating a costly, opportunistic illness is considerable for managed care plans. To hold the illness at bay, each patient requires his or her own mixture of state-of-the-art drugs. The treatments demand discipline and rigor on the part of the patient, as often twenty drugs a day must be taken at precise intervals. The cost can be extremely high. And sadly for many people, no matter how diligent they are and how much money they have expended, the treatments thus far devised aren't completely effective.

Given this background, for many people with AIDS the advent of managed care seems like just one more obstacle in a Jobian struggle to stay healthy. After all, how can a method of insurance based in part on limiting access to providers and holding down costs deal with an illness that typically generates a myriad of other medical problems, each with a need for a new specialist, new drugs, and more home care and other support? How can managed care deal with the expensive new drug protocols that may finally be winning the war against the disease, but at a cost that seems antithetical to the workings, particularly, of profit-making companies?

Those are the questions that were in the air back in 1994 when the Treatment Action Group, an AIDS lobbying organization, began the search for health insurance for its five employees. Each was HIV positive.

"The board had all five of us put our two cents in," said Peter Staley, who was then the head of the group. "What it came down to was that because of cost we would probably

IF YOU HAVE A MAJOR ILLNESS

have to go to an HMO-style plan or a hybrid. We just had to find one where all of our personal physicians were in the plan. We polled our doctors. We asked around and we used a broker."

By following these steps, Peter provided a blueprint of the basics, not just for people with AIDS, but for anyone with a serious illness: *Follow the best doctors. Ask your doctors and friends their opinions.* In many cases, there are solutions that, notwithstanding the dissatisfaction and frustration over HMO health care on the part of many people with AIDS, have brought satisfaction to many others. In the case of the Treatment Action Group, all roads led to the Freedom plan offered by Oxford Health Care. The plan's reputation for offering good doctors and an extensive formulary was strong. The primary doctors for three of the five employees were affiliated with the plan. The two employees who had to make a change were happy with the choices the plan offered. Once enrolled, the new members discovered other strengths. "Oxford has been very aggressive at signing up many specialists," Peter said. "Most of us have found that specialists we favor are in the plan."

Peter's experiences were similar to those of members of plans in California, Massachusetts, and Seattle, each of which have put themselves ahead of most others by making a commitment to aggressively developing treatment protocols for AIDS. At Peter's Oxford plan, the commitment includes several of the components that any true disease management plan should have; the plan recruited doctors specifically because of their experience in treating AIDS patients and it assigned a trained professional to look after their needs. "The great thing about Oxford that we didn't know beforehand is that the appeals process is easier for us because Oxford has a special person for AIDS, one woman with an 800 number and an extension—and she fixes things," he said. When the company Oxford uses to administer its drug formulary cut Peter's advance dosage of the protease inhibitor, Crixivan, from a thirty-day refill to a twenty-day one as part of a general policy change, Mr. Staley called her. "I said, 'That's crazy—having your supply interrupted is a very dangerous thing." He recalled that, "The AIDS woman said, 'Oh, yeah, this is not our rule, this is theirs.' She issued an exception with a phone call.' "

LESSONS TO LEARN FROM

How do you tell if the plan you are considering is as well poised as Peter's to treat your condition, or a condition you are concerned you may develop? As Peter did, find out if your primary doctor and specialists are affiliated with the plan. Ask the plan how many people with your condition are among its members. If the membership is high, the chances are, first, that there is a reason for this that reflects well on the plan's services, and, second, that even if the plan did not have a management strategy for the illness before its membership grew, in its own self interest it probably had to develop one.

For illnesses that respond well to preventive care, like heart disease, ask for a rundown of the plan's services and statistical proof of what success it has achieved. The services

IF YOU HAVE A MAJOR ILLNESS

should include cholesterol screening and strong management of diet and exercise for people most prone to heart problems. And the plans should be able to furnish you with their rates of angioplasty and bypass operations. Lower rates for each procedure can be an indication that the plan has effectively encouraged its doctors to head trouble off before it becomes critical. One key measure to inquire about involves how well a plan helps manage the care of patients after they have had a heart attack or other serious cardiac episode. Beta blockers are relatively inexpensive drugs that dramatically reduce the chances of a recurrence. Yet the rates that doctors affiliated with different plans prescribe them are dramatically different. Ask plans you are researching what their rates are. (Check the appendix A for the reported rates of many plans.)

When trying to determine how serious a plan is about its disease management system, make sure there is a contact person, preferably a nurse, who would be assigned to manage your care by coordinating primary doctors and specialists and making sure you receive the proper drugs, medical devices, and education to use them. Ask the plan to tell you the ratio of patients to such contact people to ensure you will not be dealing with an overwhelmed person installed mostly for marketing purposes. Recruitment of doctors, easy access to specialists, and an aggressive commitment to offering state-of-the-art drugs are also important barometers. To bolster AIDS treatment, for example, the Cigna Plan of Northern California has recruited three of the top doctors' groups specializing in AIDS treatment in the San Francisco Bay area. One of them receives a higher than normal capitation rate to cover the additional expenses of good AIDS care. The Health

Cooperative of Puget Sound developed a team approach, with particularly easy access to specialists and counselors. The Oxford plan and others have quickly included costly new protease inhibitors and other drugs on formularies. As Bill Thomas, an official at Cigna, said, aside from being good medicine, the drugs have shown they can reduce the need for hospitalization and thereby hold down expenses.

To help you judge programs for the illness of concern to you, call such groups as the American Cancer Society (404-320-3333), and the American Diabetes Association (703-549-1500) to find out if there are accepted national standards for illness prevention and management. And if you have the opportunity to use a point-of-service plan rather than an HMO, take it. "Definitely get out-of-network coverage, because sometime you're going to have to use it," Audrey Storch observed, after hard personal experience.

GETTING INTO A PLAN

It is important to remember that for people with complicated health histories, it is often difficult to find acceptance at any plan at all. Many plans that do accept such members establish a waiting period of between three months and two years for treatments that the plan determines are related to conditions that existed before coverage began. Given the fear and prejudice surrounding AIDS, it might appear unusual not only that Peter Staley found a plan that he is so satisfied with, but that he had several from which to choose. This is probably in no small part a reflection of special New

IF YOU HAVE A MAJOR ILLNESS

York state insurance legislation, similar to that in about a dozen other states, that lessens the hurdles to coverage for anyone with a costly medical condition. The law requires all companies that want to offer coverage to individuals or small groups to accept all applicants regardless of health status. In order to hold down rates in plans with disproportionate numbers of members with costly illnesses, New York state requires each plan to contribute to funds that are redistributed to those with the heaviest burdens.

In states without a similar program, people with serious medical problems who were not receiving coverage when their illness struck can obtain insurance through employer-run plans and sometimes on their own. But for the majority, the option is likely to be a state-designated insurance pool for the chronically ill. The problem here is usually high premiums—often barely affordable for an extensive period of time. (Indeed, even in New York, with its alternative strategy, rates are rising.) Inevitable for most people is an exhaustion of economic resources, which leads to what in some ways is a medical opportunity—qualification for Medicaid, the Federal-state program for the indigent. Each state has different qualification limits and the application process can range from short and sweet to hopelessly bureaucratic. But for illnesses such as cancer, AIDS, and heart conditions, the number of support groups in every major city is substantial, and they can help you figure out if you qualify for Medicaid and how to apply.

Medicaid itself is going through a revolution, with state after state converting its traditional fee-for-service program to managed care, inviting private insurers to provide coverage. In almost every case, the insurers are required to accept all applicants who meet Medicaid income criteria. This does not mean that subtle discrimination does not take place. Company brochures will rarely indicate that people with serious illness are welcome to apply. Sometimes the discrimination is more blatant, with company salespeople illegally asking about health status or bluntly telling would-be applicants, "This plan is not for you." These encounters should be reported to state insurance departments, whose phone numbers are listed in the appendixes.

As you work to make your best coverage decision, consider what will lead you to an experience more like Peter Staley's and less like Audrey Storch's:

[1] *Does the plan make a priority of treating your illness?* Has it developed a special protocol of best treatment options and assembled a team of doctors who have specific training and experience in treating the illness? Be aware that in some cases, plans that have developed excellent treatment modalities for serious illnesses have not publicized them widely. Critics who are active in some organizations representing people with chronic illnesses believe that these plans want to manage the diseases well for enrolled members—this cuts down on costly hospitalizations and specialist involvement—but that they don't want to attract large numbers of new patients for what, even when well managed, is costly medical care. The best plans will underscore the specialties of doctors with experience

IF YOU HAVE A MAJOR ILLNESS

in complicated costly illnesses, such as AIDS, in their printed rosters of affiliated doctors.

[2] *Does the plan allow people with serious illnesses to see specialists easily?* Needless to say, the effective treatment of such illnesses as cancer and heart disease requires a team of doctors, including a wide range of specialists, to handle the illness and the host of serious conditions that can arise as the disease progresses. Yet, in the traditional managed care procedure, every visit to a specialist must be authorized by a primary care doctor whose capitation rate comes under financial attack from a large number of referrals.

The best plans assemble teams of primary care doctors and specialists who know each other and informally or more formally work out treatment strategies for individual patients. In the most complicated cases, like AIDS, dermatologists, endocrinologists, eye, ear, nose and throat doctors, and gastroenterologists are among the specialists that are likely to be called upon as the illness progresses. The best plans allow authorizations from primary care doctors to cover several visits to a specialist usually in a fixed time period. New York state HMO regulations, which are being used as models by other states, require plans to provide standing referrals to specialists if their medical directors and the primary care physician believe they are warranted.

Some plans allow specialists to serve as primary care

doctors and others are allowing freer access to specialists. For years, the HealthPartners plan in Minnesota has allowed unlimited visits without prior approval to a wide variety of specialists in the same medical practice group as a member's primary care doctor. "We don't see any point in creating an unnecessary stopping off point for the consumer," said George Halverson, the president and chief executive officer of the 800,000 member plan. You should look for something approaching the same latitude from your plan.

[3] *Does the plan's formulary include the drugs you are dependent on? Does it include a wide range of other drugs that your doctors tell you may one day become part of your protocol, depending on how your illness develops?* After ensuring that a plan can offer you a team of doctors well versed in the treatment of your illness, there is no more important consideration in your search for a responsible plan. For many illnesses, including heart ailments, cancer, and AIDS, the most enlightened plans are anxious to list high-priced, cutting-edge drugs on their formularies. The thinking is that they can hold down even more expensive hospital stays. But there is a concern that smaller and less sophisticated HMOs and health plans operated by self-insured companies may not be as open to this. Some plans authorize the drugs soon after they are approved by the Food and Drug Administration. But others wait to do their own trials, leading to delays sometimes amounting to a half year or more.

IF YOU HAVE A MAJOR ILLNESS

If it all becomes overwhelming, check with the local chapter of your chronic illness organization, which may well have already done research on plans' drug policies. Also, find out from these groups, or from plan representatives, how open a plan is to advice from members on what drugs should be added to the formulary and what ones might look worthwhile, but could easily be removed in favor of improvements.

[4] *What measures have been taken to ensure that your problems and needs will be addressed courteously by the plan's nonmedical employees?* In a Gay Men's Health Crisis survey, the level of exasperation reached a crescendo over the difficulty many people had in getting informed answers from company phone representatives. "I got different answers every time I called—totally different answers," said one respondent who was trying to figure out how to complete some paperwork. "I filled out the form two different times with different advice. Hopefully, the second one was right." This sort of problem has led to hair pulling by HMO members of every description, but when the situation is extreme, the lack of knowledge can be more than infuriating; it can be frightening. Plans with a true commitment toward their chronically ill patients attempt to do better than this. Peter Staley's "AIDS woman" is matched in several plans by nurses who coordinate services for clusters of patients with serious illnesses. Their job is to knowledgeably answer patients' queries and cut through the red tape in filling

prescriptions, contacting specialists, making appeals of coverage denials, and answering everyday questions about the issues and problems that come up. The presence or absence of such people says a lot about a plan's commitment to managing your illness.

[5] *What are the plan's annual and lifetime ceilings on drug and other medical expenditures?* Almost every plan imposes a limit on how much it will pay for drugs, hospital care, and the like. The breakthrough combinations of drugs that promise to turn AIDS into a manageable illness for many people and to curtail other illnesses are very costly and subject to frequent change and augmentation. This promises to push members of many plans over the coverage limits. Safety net plans run by many states may provide some degree of support when the ceiling is hit, but it is very important to read the fine print that separates one plan from another to make sure that you haven't signed on for limitations on coverage that are unnecessarily tight.

[6.] *How does the plan define experimental treatments that fall outside the bounds of coverage?* Every plan places limits on what medical procedures it will cover, thereby protecting itself against huge expenditures for procedures that, however critical members believe they are, often have little or no proven track records. The definition of what is experimental, however, can vary from plan to plan, with some adopting the judgments of the Medicare program and others relying on the determinations of their own, often more conserva-

IF YOU HAVE A MAJOR ILLNESS

tive, medical advisory boards. The difference in interpretation can mean the difference between being covered and being rejected for a procedure that you and your doctor believe is necessary.

[7] *Does the plan cover reasonable visits to the emergency room, even when it later turns out that the member's condition was not a medical emergency?* This is a perennial issue for managed care plans and one of special concern to people with serious illnesses who are likely to develop a host of symptoms, often extremely painful, that could justifiably send them racing to the nearest hospital emergency room. It used to be standard for plans to require most patients to call for authorization as soon as they are able to do so—in many cases they have been asked to receive authorization *before* receiving treatment. It was also standard for plans to refuse to pay for treatments later deemed to have been nonemergency in nature. Among all the contentious policies of managed care plans, few have generated more anger than this one. It asks members to seemingly do the impossible—wait for authorization when they are in extemis—and to undertake a risk that most Americans undoubtedly look at as unfair, if not unconscionable—to pay for their own care if in retrospect it is deemed to be nonemergency in nature.

Several states have outlawed these sorts of provisions. All things considered, you should do your best to avoid plans that still have emergency room requirements that put too heavy a burden on you. Under great pressure, many plans have adopted a "prudent layperson" standard. As defined by the American College of Emergency Physicians, any condition would qualify as an emergency if it were "of recent onset and severity that would lead a 'prudent layperson,' possessing an average knowledge of medicine and health, to believe that urgent and/or unscheduled medical care is required." Your plan should offer nothing less.

| 10 |

MENTAL HEALTH CONSIDERATIONS

For Cindy Parks, psychotherapy was a lifeline to a more hopeful future. In an abusive relationship for a dozen years, she talked through her problems and her underlying personality patterns for two and a half years with her therapist before she could contemplate breaking off her relationship and begin to plot it out legally and in a way she felt safe. For those who have dealt with similarly sensitive situations, the time frame of her therapy is unlikely to seem excessive: It took Cindy more than a year to feel trusting enough in her therapist to bring up the more painful aspects of her life.

But as she was preparing to end the relationship, her

Boston-based employer switched from a fee-for-service plan to a managed care plan. Cindy's problem was that her therapist was not affiliated with the new plan. "I went into deep depression," she recalled. Her new plan offered her a therapist, but she declined to see him because he was not a licensed psychologist. She began missing work and called the plan's 800 mental health number for stopgap counseling. She was told the phone personnel couldn't help her because her problems were affecting her work and were therefore too severe to be dealt with in that ad hoc manner. She was given another number to call, but came to feel that, at a time when she needed support and guidance, she was getting a bureaucratic runaround, and the therapeutic setting she had worked to make her own would never be replicated in this new environment.

In the end, she decided to get the help she needed by going outside the plan and incurring a debt of $12,000.

REVOLUTION IN MENTAL HEALTH CARE

Cindy Parks's experience is far from unique. Managed care has done more to lower employers' mental health expenses than any other element of their health costs. Mental health accounted for 10 percent of employers' costs in 1988. By 1995, they were down to 4 percent of the costs. The question is, How much has managed care deprived patients of needed treatment in the process? How much has it led them, in frustration, to seek help on their own? And for the

MENTAL HEALTH CONSIDERATIONS

person looking to choose health coverage wisely, is there a way to ensure that treatment needs can be met?

Roughly 150 million Americans—those with current psychological needs and those without them—receive their mental health coverage through managed care. An estimated five million Americans have to contend with serious mental problems in the course of a year. Another 35 million have lesser, but still significant problems. Yet, mental health needs traditionally have never received the respect given to the provision of acute physical care. As a result, the massive transformation that managed care has caused in the delivery of mental health services has barely drawn significant attention.

Indeed, if managed care has revolutionized medical care in general, it has had perhaps its most profound effect in the area of mental health. Here it has altered not simply how services are delivered, but the nature of the services themselves. Treatment of mental ailments is far less likely than treatment of physical conditions to take place during protracted hospital stays. Traditional "talk therapy," in which a patient explores the root causes of a problem over months or years, is reimbursed only in the rarest of cases. Drug therapy has largely taken its place, to the consternation of many mental health professionals.

To the extent that analysis remains covered, it is for a rigidly fixed number of sessions, perhaps a couple or a half dozen, and targeted to a tightly defined problem, which most often prevents a person from functioning well at work—substance abuse or depression, for example. Where the sensitive details of a patient's condition were once largely a private matter between client and therapist, mental health professionals now regularly complain that managed care companies ask for personal information that should never leave their offices. And stories abound of patients like Cindy Parks, who absorb the full cost of their treatment rather than fill out the forms many companies require for payment.

CARVE-OUT COMPANIES

In the great majority of cases, managed care companies don't handle mental health coverage directly. Instead they subcontract it to one of a half dozen large companies, called "carve-out companies," which provide the lion's share of mental health services received through health plans. Representatives of these companies are well aware of the complaints leveled against them by therapists and patients. Some executives acknowledge mistakes in denying coverage but assert that they are the responsibility of a few bad apple firms or that they are no more prevalent than they had been under any previous form of insurance. Meanwhile, they claim, they have managed to hold down costs that got out of control under fee-for-service medicine. They also maintain that they have created some sense of discipline in a field where critics have always contended that success is hard to measure and pointless "treatments" have been carried out and paid for for too long.

To do this, managed care companies have devised a wide variety of tougher and more restrictive monitoring processes.

MENTAL HEALTH CONSIDERATIONS

Plan members generally have to call a toll free number to request treatment. Typically, they have to report their symptoms and other personal information to an intake worker, who not infrequently has no mental health training. In many cases, this person consults guidelines set down by a plan and determines whether the symptoms described qualify for coverage. If the symptoms are deemed to qualify, the case folder, in many plans, is sent on to a second caseworker, this one with mental health training and experience, who decides whether the symptoms warrant treatment by a social worker, psychologist, or, in the most extreme cases, a psychiatrist, who by degree can prescribe medications.

Many plans require the therapist to furnish a written treatment strategy within twenty-four hours, geared to the alleviation of conditions that are, most often, thought to be the cause of very specific problems at work, like repeated absence, tardiness, or inability to complete tasks. Prozac and other drugs are often chosen in place of traditional talk therapy. And the talk therapy sessions are usually approved in modest units of two or three sessions. Many plans report that most therapy encounters end in five or six sessions, the time that numerous traditional talk therapists say it takes them to build trust with new patients and begin to determine a rounded diagnosis.

For patients seeking hospitalization, the hurdles can be just as arduous, with pre-approval required in all but the most extreme cases. In cases where a doctor admits a patient and the plan disputes the decision, it is typically the patient's family that is liable for the bill. Appeals are permitted of denials of either inpatient or outpatient care, but many therapists say that patients are often scared away by the prospect of having their case histories turned over to a review board.

The effects on hospitalization have been dramatic. In the '70s, the average psychiatric patient was admitted for twenty-five days. The average stay these days for managed care patients is about five days. To be sure, other factors are responsible for this extraordinary change—new therapy strategies, drug breakthroughs, legitimate rectification of the waste and abuse of the past. But it is indisputable that much is due to the intensity of review that marks managed care and in particular, the carve-out companies on the front lines.

WHAT THIS MEANS FOR THE PATIENT

These companies and the theorists who broadly support their efforts can point to several reasons for the extensive reviews and the transformation they have wrought. Psychotherapy, they argue, was allowed to run amok during the '70s and '80s. Even with co-payments that ran as high as 50 percent and ceilings on payments of $50,000 or $100,000, enormous costs were shifted onto the insurance system, raising premiums for all. Many therapists, the plans argue, use outdated methodologies. And, too often, they say, employers inappropriately pay for deep personal analysis when they should only be responsible for correcting symptoms that impair worker performance.

Therapists, of course, dispute all of this vehemently, but for a person trying to make a determination of which of a

MENTAL HEALTH CONSIDERATIONS

limited number of plans to join, the debate does little more than provide a cautionary context for a difficult decision. Making the choice all the more tough is the fact that many people who will eventually require or request therapeutic help don't have a history of having done so in the past.

If you have no history, how important is it for you to consider mental health services in making an overall decision about a plan? And, with carve-out companies determining the bulk of a plan's mental health policies, is it even possible to know what you are signing on for? The carve-out companies have undergone tremendous consolidation and upheaval. Thus, the carve-out company dictating a managed care plan's policies now may not be the one executing them at your time of need.

Nonetheless, there are points to keep in mind when choosing a plan and when facing a mental health crisis. They can make the difference between effective treatment and a limiting and frustrating attempt at getting help.

[1] *If you need help, take stock of options available outside the health insurance arena.* Does your company have an employee assistance program? Most big ones do and many of them are enormously effective in situations far more varied than those with which these plans are usually associated, such as substance abuse and depression. They are regularly consulted by employees grappling with difficult work situations and personal problems like divorce and the illness of a loved one. It is the professional code of employee as-

sistance plans that any information discussed with the plan's counselors is kept confidential, unknown even to the company itself.

Indeed, it is the general policy of the plans that they do not inform the company that an employee has even sought help. If a supervisor refers you for help, though, it is standard for this to be recorded in your personnel folder. And employees may also choose to let their companies know of their request for help to account for absences from work and to show their good faith in dealing with problems when they arise.

Churches, synagogues, and community organizations often offer counseling programs of their own. Group therapy sessions can run as low as fifteen dollars a week (although they can run as high as five times this amount) and provide enormous support and guidance. For those willing to undertake the expense, private therapy is always an option that allows you to have total decision-making in your hands. Depending on which area of the country you live in and the background and training of your therapist, fifty minute sessions can run between $35 and $150.

[2] *Ask whether your health plan administers its own mental health coverage or whether it carves it out for servicing by a behavioral health specialty company.* The difference is important for a few reasons. First, many of the plans that run their own mental health programs are long-standing not-for-profit organizations that by-and-large have received relatively strong ratings from their

MENTAL HEALTH CONSIDERATIONS

members. Second, the integration of mental health coverage into the plan's total strategy allows for important synergism.

The HMO Group, a consortium of not-for-profit plans, for example, is sponsoring a trial program in which member plans train their primary care doctors to detect the symptoms of depression. While on its face, this seems a sound practice medically, it is more than that. Dan Wolfson, president of the group, believes it will make a case for itself with employers by showing that by dealing with depression up front, costly treatment of physical ailments will decrease.

Third, managed care plans frequently change carve out-companies. Thus, the rules that were in effect when you joined a managed care plan may change radically by the time you need help—and this is important to bear in mind when deciding between options.

[3] *Find out whether the managed care company you are considering offers a point-of-service option that allows you to go to therapists who are not affiliated with the plan.* While this is an important issue for every kind of health care, it is particularly important for those with mental health concerns. This is because members of any HMO who are seeking help for a physical problem can choose primary care doctors and specialists from a thick list of physician affiliates. It is standard for members looking for mental health services to receive a list of three therapists who are within a nearby geographic range. The particular approach of those

therapists—whether short- or long-term, drug or talk based, reliant on hospitalization or outpatient care—is not specified. If you find one therapist's philosophy or manner are not to your liking, you have only two other possible opportunities.

With a point-of-service plan, however, you can find the therapist of your choice, which is key, and cover your analysis through co-payments and a deductible. Total freedom, though, is not a characteristic of this approach either. Your therapist will most likely still have to submit detailed reports to the health plan and await approval for reimbursement for the prescribed course of treatment.

[4] *Don't underestimate the importance of privacy issues, which might seem far removed when you are making a health plan choice but can become paramount at a time of need.* Every managed care plan asks questions about your diagnosis and treatment plan after you first see a therapist. Some ask for far more information than others, including personal histories and detailed descriptions of the immediate causes of psychic stress.

One large carve-out company, for example, uses a form requiring therapists to report on more than forty possible symptoms and issues, including suicide and homicide risk, spousal and substance abuse, and sexual dysfunctions. Plans usually approve therapy sessions in clusters as low as two and seldom higher than five or six; each time a therapist believes more sessions are

MENTAL HEALTH CONSIDERATIONS

warranted, he or she is required to fill out another report.

Often it is the patient, as well, who has to provide detailed information by filling out forms when applying for therapeutic services. In addition, review officers from the plan may appear from time to time at the clinician's office to review notes of treatment. On top of this, if a patient wants to appeal a denial of treatment by a plan, still more information is usually required to back up the case; enough, in some cases, for the plan member to feel that the process is so intrusive it is better to abandon the appeal effort.

To the plans, these reviews and checks are vital—they claim they help them determine whether proven treatment initiatives are being followed by practitioners who frequently have had limited or no oversight. Therapists, of course, complain of second guessing by people with fewer credentials and less experience than they have—one former employee of Massachusetts Blue Cross claimed in an affidavit taken in connection with a suit against the company that he regularly fielded calls on a hot line from distraught, sometimes hysterical people, even though he had little in the way of training to prepare him for such encounters. (The plan disputes mistreating members with mental health problems and said the ex-employee "lacks credibility" and was cited for excessive lateness and absences.)

But beyond the issue of the immediate use that the information is put to is the question of what happens to all of it after it has been supplied. Do you want a number of caseworkers and utilization review officers pouring over your life history? Is there a chance that the information can wind up on your employer's desk, as some therapists have contended happens on occasion? Can it find its way into divorce proceedings or other public arenas? There have been instances, according to many therapists, where caseworkers have openly gossiped about information and where job promotions and divorce disputes have been influenced by this information.

Plans argue that they only ask for the minimum amount of information necessary for an evaluation and they store it in secure computer systems that rival the Pentagon's. But you should not rest on these assurances. If mental health is a concern, ask to see the informational forms required of you and your therapist. And remember that there may be other settings where information is requested as well, like emergency rooms, where intake officers may ask you detailed questions to assure that the hospital will receive compensation for treatment from your health plan. After joining, ask the therapist to go over the forms with you. Find out who the form goes to and ask if your employer might receive the information—larger plans absolutely deny they ever share information, but suspicions remain that smaller plans may not be as rigorous. For one dollar each, you can receive two publications from The American Health Information Management Association, at 800-335-5535; *Your Health Information*

MENTAL HEALTH CONSIDERATIONS

Belongs to You, and *Is Your Health Information Confidential?* The organization maintains a website at www.ahima.org.

[5] *Carefully match the financial fine print of different plans.* After years of inequality, all must offer the same lifetime benefit for mental health coverage as they do for coverage of physical health. But this equity notwithstanding, there are wide variations among plans. Employer-sponsored plans are exempt from this legislation and may still offer ceilings as high as $1 million for physical coverage and only $50,000 to $100,000 for mental coverage. Disparities can still be considerable in other areas, too. Plans have annual caps on how much they will cover in mental health coverage. These can vary greatly, as can the number of covered outpatient visits a year. At one point, for example, the large HealthNet plan in California allowed for fifty visits a year, while others allowed only twenty, a figure HealthNet has slipped back to, citing as a reason recent legislation requiring parity in the value of mental and physical health benefits.

Even these gross figures can be deceptive. Find out what services they cover. At some plans they include simple medication checks as well as private therapy sessions. Further, while the plan's guidelines may permit twenty, or even fifty, visits, this does not mean in practice it will authorize nearly that many for most diagnoses. For the set of symptoms you present, only a half dozen visits might be allowed, regardless of what the plan's cap is. And, on top of this, if you are in a point-of-service plan, your annual dollar cap may run out before your number of visits do.

[6] *Find out what your freedom of choice is regarding style of treatment before joining a plan.* If you are directed by a plan to a clinician who believes in drug therapy and you do not, do you have the option of declining treatment and finding another practitioner more to your liking? If you do, what precisely is the process that enables you to do this?

[7] *If you are dependent on a psychotropic drug, find out if it is on a plan's formulary and, if possible, how often that formulary is prone to change.* If the plan offers a generic version of a brand drug you are reliant on, ask your doctor whether there is a history of patients reacting to the generic version differently than the brand version.

[8] *Consider what your real objectives are in seeking out therapy.* If they involve a broad analysis of the underpinnings of your personality, managed care—employer-sponsored managed care, in particular—may not be the right setting for you. Consider the subtle difference in these responses to the same question at the end of a long discussion of managed care published in *The Wall Street Journal,* which Cindy Parks, as a frustrated patient, participated in. "What is successful treatment?" the panel moderator asked. Dr. Peter Panzarino, a psychiatrist and medical director of Vista Health Plans, a large behavioral health carve-out com-

MENTAL HEALTH CONSIDERATIONS

pany based in San Diego, responded: "It's a reduction of symptoms that brought someone into treatment and a return to the level of functioning he or she had before the acute (psychological) crisis occurred. Successful treatment also gives people skills for living that enable them to handle similar situations more effectively in the future."

A different answer came from a strong critic of the way managed care deals with mental health needs—Dr. Karen Shore, a psychologist and president of the National Coalition of Mental Health Consumers and Professionals: "It is when a person can understand himself and his world enough to be able to meet the demands of adult life—and find satisfaction."

Dr. Panzarino's reaction stressed response to a single psychological episode and a return to functioning at the pre-episode level. Dr. Shore's response emphasized reaching a deeper self-understanding as a foundation for overall functioning and enjoyment of life. Her definition may be a particularly rich and resonant one, but many employers argue that it describes something far outside their orbit. They say they are willing to pay a portion of the cost it takes to help an employee function and be productive at work, but that deeper mental health concerns fall outside their responsibility. (Some companies, like Hewlett-Packard, which allow thirty-one visits a year feel quite strongly to the contrary.)

For those consumers seeking more than a quick Band-Aid at a time of crisis, for those who worry about privacy considerations, for those who fear that the financial interests of plan and employer work against treatment considerations, going Cindy Parks's route—that is undertaking therapy privately—may be the best course. Of course, it can be extremely expensive. But there are alternatives that can ease the financial stress. There are still fee-for-service plans that will cover private therapy, usually with a 50 percent co-payment. And there are clinics run by graduate and medical schools, where treatment can be had for as little as five or ten dollars a session. Student clinicians receive professional supervision.

| 11 |

STANDING UP
FOR YOUR RIGHTS

It was mid-1996 when Linda Gibbs found herself confronting the crisis of her life; a spreading, extremely advanced ovarian cancer that required immediate surgery and a rigorous regimen of chemotherapy. The treatment worked and, for a while, the cancer was forced into remission. A year later, though, Linda received more bad news. Doctors identified another cancerous growth, which they removed from her chest. As distressing, they determined that the ovarian cancer again had begun to grow and spread.

Linda's primary care doctor and her gynecological cancer specialist, both affiliated with her managed care company,

Oxford Health Plans, recommended an extreme type of treatment to save her life—a high-dosage form of chemotherapy and a form of bone marrow transplant called a stem cell transplant. Each is hugely expensive and has been used in the rarest of ovarian cases, but Linda's doctors felt it was the best shot left for a vibrant woman in her forties who had already responded well to chemotherapy and had the strength to endure painful and exhausting treatments. Last June 23, Oxford rejected Linda's request, dismissing the procedures as unproven, unlikely to be more effective than conventional treatments, and possibly injurious to her health. Her only recourse was to appeal the decision to the plan's appeals coordinator. This set off an all-out offensive by Linda, who in a letter to Oxford a week later cautioned, "Please do not underestimate the aggressive force I will bring to this appeals process. As you must know by now, this is a matter of life and death." Linda's experience over the next ten days can serve as a model for those fighting to get service after it has been rejected by a plan.

WHEN COVERAGE IS DENIED

Perhaps the most agonizing aspect of managed care—or any form of insurance—is the denial of a request for coverage for a seriously ill person. In a world of limited resources, it is impossibly and inadvisably costly to approve every request for every form of treatment. Medical directors and other plan officials have to make difficult decisions that win them few friends, but are often proper and even courageous. But

STANDING UP FOR YOUR RIGHTS

within the world of review and rejection is the unsettling mix of medicine and money. The most cutting-edge and, proportionately, most frequently rejected procedures are extremely costly, leaving the inevitable suspicion that a plan is protecting its bottom line quite literally at the expense of its members' health or lives.

As a measure of due process, every plan offers some sort of appeals process, which allows a second look at denials of coverage. Some are far more evolved than others, including outside doctors in the review panel, appointing ombudsmen or case managers to help patients through the process, and broadcasting widely that such a process even exists. Proposed laws across the country would require the process to go even further, establishing outside review boards with no links to any plan that would be truly independent appeals panels, and permitting for greater access to the courts.

PLANNING YOUR BATTLE

The process Linda Gibbs had to contend with was less arms length than this. Oxford operated its own appeals process, which began for the member with a written notice sent to the medical management appeals coordinator. It was with a letter to the registered nurse who held this position that Linda began the fight of her life. Vowing to press her appeal, Linda wrote that she was "outraged, dismayed, and appalled" by the rejection. "I have three fine physicians who all agree that I am the perfect candidate for this procedure," she stated.

She backed this letter up with lengthy letters from all three doctors. In one, her gynecological oncologist recalled their history together, which began in March 1996 when Linda was so short of breath and experiencing such intense abdominal pain that she rushed her straight to the hospital. She described the research she did before recommending the stem cell transplant—consulting with doctors at Johns Hopkins, Tufts, and Loyola Universities and the National Cancer Institute. And she cited recent studies that indicated that although clinical trials had not been completed, the use of high-dose chemotherapy and stem cell transplants were likely to be far more effective than realized for some ovarian cancer patients. "I have very rarely recommended this therapy to a patient with ovarian cancer, because in most cases it is unlikely to change long-term outcome," she wrote. "It appears that she is the optimal patient for high-dose therapy."

With financial help from friends and family, Linda also hired a lawyer, Mark Scherzer, who, as a legislative aide, was a key author of New York State's managed care bill of rights. In a carefully argued five-page letter, he challenged the plan's decision on procedural and legal grounds, concluding that if Linda did not win a reversal from the plan, she reserved, "the right to pursue all other available avenues for enforcing her coverage under the policy, including complaints to the insurance department and litigation."

Finally, relying again on the assistance of friends and family members, she wrote for help to a number of public officials. Writing to Oxford on her behalf were U.S. Senators Daniel Patrick Moynihan and Alfonse D'Amato and State Assemblymen Steve Sanders and Pete Grannis. Grannis, the chairman of the Assembly's Insurance Committee, had been critical of Oxford for long delays in making its reimbursements to doctors and hospitals. He was particularly forceful. "It seems to me this is exactly the type of health care—cautious, prudent, and well-informed, with the patient's best interest at heart—that Oxford should be embracing," he wrote.

In a three-sentence letter to her dated July 7, 1997, Oxford informed Linda that it had decided to reverse its decision. It didn't specify why and it is unclear which parts of her onslaught had the greatest effect on the plan. A few weeks later, in her words, she "sailed through" the procedure. Her cancer went into remission, although her health has to be monitored regularly and the arduous protocol sapped her strength, which she is still working to fully regain.

LESSONS TO BE LEARNED

There is much to be learned from Linda's dogged battle to get the kind of care she and her doctors believed she needed. Her experience opens the window on that of thousands of health plan members who find the course of treatment recommended by their doctors rejected for coverage. In a significant number of cases, the rejections apply to cutting-edge procedures that to the patient hold a last chance that a mortal illness can be routed or thrown into remission. But in many others they can involve coverage denials that while not of life or death proportions are nonetheless of great importance to plan members—a rejection over a referral to a specialist, the use of a drug not on the plan's formulary, or a surgical procedure that the member's doctor believes would be highly useful.

There are still many plans that make appealing such a decision far more difficult than it ought to be. The appeals process is mentioned in every plan's benefit package material, usually in fine print and in language that can be hard to understand. A plan's appeals process—how well developed it is, how concerted the plan's efforts to publicize its existence are—is a telltale sign of overall quality and commitment to members. Oftentimes the appeal reviews are undertaken behind closed doors by the plan's own medical director or review personnel. Even when there is some distance between the review process and the plan, the appeals panel will usually include plan representatives and, quite often, personnel involved in the original rejection of coverage, raising clear conflict of interest issues.

It is for this reason that many of the managed care reform bills proposed in Congress and on the state level include provisions for completely independent review panels and greater recourse to the courts. There is little doubt that these panels will become more and more prevalent over the years for at least the most serious procedures. They will no doubt add to the cost of running a health plan and probably the cost of coverage, as well, but they speak to a basic American sense of fairness and justice.

As matters stand now, however, members can fight for what they need in a number of different ways, some of them reflective of a sophisticated understanding of the appeals process, others of an understanding of all the outside pres-

STANDING UP FOR YOUR RIGHTS

sures that can be brought to bear on a publicly regulated company. If you have been denied coverage you think you are entitled to, keep these steps in mind:

[1] *File an appeals notice immediately.* By now most, but not all plans, include information about how to file an appeal with a notice of denial of coverage. In the majority of states, they are required to do so. Many plans, sometimes in accordance with state law, accept oral notices of appeal from members, which are supposed to be logged in when they arrive. But even if you file one orally, back it up with a written notice, sent by registered mail.

If the coverage denial affects a service that can have an immediate impact on your health, ask for an expedited review. Many plans will speed the review of denials in cases considered "urgent care situations" or ones where a doctor believes the denial will lead to an emergency health situation. North Carolina law requires a review to begin within three days after a request in expedited situations and a decision rendered one business day after all the information for review is submitted. Wisconsin requires a decision within four business days after an appeal is filed. The public interest group Families USA has compiled a list of state regulations that can tell you what your state has legislated. Each state also has one, or sometimes two, agencies charged with monitoring health plans. A list of them and their phone numbers appear in appendix E.

[2] *Consult your contract or membership benefits package to understand the inner workings of the appeals process.* Look for details about the timetable for the various steps, the information that may be considered by reviewers, whether you can appear and testify personally at a hearing, and the definitions the plan uses to determine whether a procedure or service is covered. The variation between plans on each of these factors can be extreme. Under state law, for example, Vermont requires grievances to be decided within fifteen days unless there are extenuating circumstances. Under Virginia law, according to Families U.S.A., plans have had as long as 180 days—enough time to render the final decision academic in many cases.

In each state, individual plans also vary widely in terms of speed of response. Under Missouri law, there is a detailed timetable that must be observed: acknowledgment of receipt of an appeal within ten days and a completed investigation within twenty days unless there are exceptional circumstances, which must be explained to the member within thirty days. In many plans, there is a two step appeals process. The first step usually involves an appeal to a medical director or another officer of the plan, sometimes the very one who denied coverage to begin with. If this results in an affirmation of the denial, a more involved process comes into play. A member can appeal again, usually to a full board, which may or may not include the plan official who made the original decision. The structure of these boards varies greatly. The best plans will keep anyone with a prior involvement in the case off the appeals board, and some plans will include representation from other plan members. Illinois, in fact, requires that members make up half the composition of every grievance panel.

Many plans will allow you to personally argue your case before an appeals board and to present a wide range of medical and personal information. Be sure to document your condition and the reasonableness of the treatment you are requesting to the fullest. As Elaine Hamilton, who has worked as a benefits manager for several companies in northern California, says, "You have to be the intelligent educator to the insurance company of why your condition is an exception."

[3] *Rely on support from others.* As Linda Gibbs showed, your doctors should be important allies in your appeal. It is their medical judgment that is being rejected by the plan and they should be called on to defend it. In many cases, doctors will step to the fore and lead the way, out of concern for their patients and anger over being second guessed in ways they consider inappropriate. In many plans, backed by law in several states, doctors and other health care providers are allowed to file their own grievances with a plan over coverage denials pertaining to their patients. In the best plans, members can rely on help from the plan itself, in the form of a personally assigned case manager who gener-

ally has no prior involvement in a member's case and whose job it is to guide the patient through the appeals process as effectively as possible.

[4] *Look for help outside the plan.* Linda Gibbs provides a textbook example of where to go. She retained a savvy lawyer who not only wrote a detailed letter in her support that cited medical precedent and case law but who also intimated that, unless overturned, her plan's denial would be a subject for the courts and the state insurance department. In several states, like Florida, plan members are allowed to file grievances with state supervisory agencies at any stage of the appeals process, with the state empowered to order treatment in cases where it has been denied. In more states, the supervising state agency is explicitly sanctioned to review cases upon request after they have made their way through a plan's internal appeals process. And in every other state, this means of appeal is open, even if it hasn't been laid out explicitly by law.

The process, of course, can add more time to the wait for treatment. And in some states consumers have complained that because of a lack of publicity most health plan members don't even know the option is available. But thousands of people have benefited by going to their states, and the simple threat to do so is a powerful lever for plan members. Your state insurance department should be able to tell you who to write to to kick off the process. Beyond the state agency lies the courts. Challenging a plan's decision can take time

STANDING UP FOR YOUR RIGHTS

and money—and sometimes plan members have inadvertently signed away their right to do so. This issue reached a white heat in California over the standard provision in many Kaiser Permanente plans, which is used by several other large plans as well, which requires members to agree to forgo recourse to the courts in favor of the plan's arbitration process. The practice led to an adverse court decision against Kaiser and movements to outlaw such provisions as violations of plan members' due process.

But the court process is a complicated and costly one that should not be undertaken without a competent lawyer who is well versed in the specialty of insurance law. In addition, Federal judges around the country have ruled that members do not have recourse to the courts if their plans are employer-sponsored and regulated in Washington. At press time, this was the subject of keen debate in Congress. The real hope for most litigants is that the time and expense—coupled with the possibility in some cases of bad publicity—will cause the plan to offer an out-of-court settlement that can help defray a good chunk of your medical expenses.

Elaine Hamilton, the benefits adviser from northern California, for example, sued her managed care plan after receiving a denial of coverage for an innovative procedure to correct a skeletal deformity of the chest that was threatening her twelve-year-old son's health and growth. After receiving the rejection, the Hamilton family paid $30,000 privately to have the procedure undertaken at Stanford University Medical Center. The results were miraculous, with her son Sam growing six inches in a year and becoming a high school athlete. The plan settled her suit out-of-court for $20,000—and the promise that she not use its name in talking about her experience.

[5] *Don't underestimate the role of friends, contacts, and even politicians.* In immeasurable ways, some of your strongest help can come from people who don't have any legal or official link to your case, but who have the clout to command a plan's attention. Faced with the possibility that the last best chance at routing her cancer was being denied, Linda Gibbs turned to friends and family. They sent synopses of her condition to any politician in New York State who they thought could help. To the letters from Linda's doctors and lawyer, Oxford could add appeals from a host of prominent officeholders.

| 12 |

TAKING CONTROL

A couple of years ago, Mark Green, as the elected public administrator in New York City, assembled a team of researchers for a lengthy study of HMO coverage in the city. He had them call up each of the local managed care plans and request information from phone representatives. Their results would have been startling only to people who have never dealt with health plan phone representatives. At one plan, the Health Insurance Plan of New York (HIP), the wait was usually at least ten minutes before a customer service representative finally responded to the call, a problem the plan says it has since corrected. At others the wait was frequently more than five minutes.

Once representatives were available, they often gave inaccurate and conflicting information. For example, representatives of Travelers Insurance and U.S. Healthcare told the callers they had up to forty-eight hours after an emergency room episode to call for approval. In fact, the plans required a call within twenty-four hours. The same question, asked of three different representatives at Aetna yielded three different responses. How many visits to a specialist is a primary care doctor's referral good for? the phone representatives were asked. One, was the answer from one representatives, four or five the answer from another, and five or six the answer from the third.

FRUSTRATIONS OF A SYSTEM IN FLUX

The results were likely a disturbing reflection of many factors in the health insurance field, none of them good for the consumer—the rapid pace of health plan mergers and changes in ownership, poor personnel training programs, and the staffing of customer relations positions with recent college graduates with little experience in health care or benefits management.

This lack of reliability when requesting information, as disturbing as it is in its own right, is but one indication of a bigger problem for many plan members. When they are seeking help, their health plans can very often seem to be standing in the way. There are certainly plans that are consistently competent and professional in caring for their members' needs for information, guidance, and quick reimbursement. But it pays to deal with your plan as if it isn't. All members should be vigilant and treat encounters with their plans cautiously. This means it is essential to call your plan's 800 service number any time you are uncertain about what your coverage allows—whether it is a change of primary care doctors, an emergency room visit, a trip to a hospital out of your service area, or a reimbursement that has been denied or is late in coming. It is also important to keep a log of these encounters and record the time and date, the name of the service representative, and the advice given. For critical information, ask that your questions be answered in writing.

But to ensure that you get what you are entitled to with a minimum of hassle, your preparation should begin far before your call. This does not have to be a life project or a product of HMO paranoia. By doing a bit of research and relying on allies that you might ordinarily overlook, your relations with your plan stand a greater chance of being as straightforward and unconfusing as they ought to be.

[1] *Start a health insurance file beginning with your contract and the package of explanatory information that plans provide when you join up.* These documents include the details about what services are covered and how the plan's procedures work. The general problem with them is they often read as if they were written by

lawyers rather than people trying to impart information in a clear way. As Peter Fox, an experienced health plan consultant, says, "I find it hard to understand them myself."

Still, if you have a question about whether a particular service is covered, how to change your primary care doctor, or how to dispute a rejected claim, consult your written references first. Sometimes the information will speak for itself, usually in describing whether services like home care or certain types of medical equipment are covered, and in describing simple bureaucratic procedures, like how to change your primary care doctor.

At other times, they provide you with language and a written reference that you can take to the plan's service representatives. Asking for clarification of a particular passage is usually more fruitful than a generalized question that a representative might misunderstand or interpret incorrectly.

[2] *Ask your employer for help.* In a great many cases, companies are self-insured and use health plans only to administer a program that they have set up and financed. In other cases, the companies are major clients of health plans. Either way, your employer, particularly if medium- or large-sized, may well be a voice your health plan has to listen to. If you have a question or a problem that is not being resolved, ask your company's benefits department for help. Often, a benefits officer will make a call for you or put you in touch

with a service representative specifically assigned to the company account.

[3] *Ask your doctor or hospital for help.* If you are confused about whether a service recommended by your doctor falls under your coverage, your doctor may be able to clarify this for you with a call. If you want to change physicians, your prospective doctor should be able to explain the procedure. The same goes for many hospitals that have treated you under emergency circumstances. Their customer service departments are anxious to collect their bills and your insurance plan has the deepest pockets. The hospital has probably dealt with your plan before and knows what it requires before authorizing payment.

[4] *Keep copies of every bill you send to your health plan and every response you receive from it.* This helps establish a documentary record, which can help you press your claim for payment after it has been denied. My family learned this lesson in dealing with a point-of-service plan run by Prudential. As is often the case, we had no problem when we stuck with doctors on the plan's panel, but when we ventured outside, it seemed that many a government agency knew how to process forms far more efficiently than this plan. Procedures that phone representatives assured my wife were covered were continually rejected for reimbursement. This led to more phone calls with other representatives, who reaffirmed that the bills would be taken care of. Three or four times over, they weren't. But

after more than half a year of perseverance, the claims—$300 of them—were paid. Without the paper trail of rejected claims and the names of the service representatives (always get the name of the person you talk to) who had confirmed their qualification for payment, the process, at the least, would undoubtedly have been tougher.

[5] *When you have been denied coverage you think you are entitled to, you can always appeal the decision through the plan's internal hearing mechanism.* The preceding chapter talks about appeals issues in depth, but at the least you should know that plans must offer you a court of last resort and that the best ones will put you in contact with a plan representative who will help you argue your side of the case. As the managed care system evolves further, more and more states are beginning to contemplate mandating independent appeals processes removed from the plans. But for now it is best to understand how to work the current systems as best as you can.

[6] *If you and your doctor are convinced that a service is absolutely necessary and your plan refuses to cover it, try to figure out a way to finance the procedure anyway.* If your health is at stake, take care of it first if you can and fight the plan later over payment.

[7] *Be prepared to leave an unsatisfactory plan.* If you look back at months of mixed signals from phone representatives, late reimbursements, and general aggravation

TAKING CONTROL

and confusion, vote with your feet and leave the plan during the next enrollment period. Membership in a health plan is not like a marriage. If you are self-employed or work for a company that offers multiple options, you can switch to new coverage every year.

APPENDIX A

The National Committee for Quality Assurance is the nation's largest accreditation agency for health plans. A nonprofit group governed by a board of health care experts, consumers, employers, labor unions, and health plans, the NCQA has put more than three hundred plans through evaluations designed to determine whether they have systems in place to encourage the health of their members by promoting quality medical practices. The organization also monitors how well the plans provide important medical services. The two charts in this appendix display many of the agency's important determinations and findings.

The first chart lists the accreditation status of plans relying on the most recent information through the end of June 1998. *Full* accreditation is granted for three years to plans judged to have met the agency's performance standards and to have superior programs that encourage continuous quality improvement. *One-year* accreditation is given to plans that meet most NCQA standards and have established quality improvement programs. After a year, the agency reviews the plans again to determine whether they now merit full accreditation. *Provisional* accreditation is granted for a year to plans that meet some NCQA standards and have adequate quality improvement programs. Plans that fail to meet standards are *denied* accreditation.

Because of the agency's heavy schedule of evaluations and reevaluations, a plan's status may have changed by the time you read this. You can check on the accreditation status of a plan at any time by calling 888-275-7585. You can also consult the NCQA web site at www.ncqa.org.

The second chart lists the performance of hundreds of plans on important quality measures that the organization monitors. High scores indicate good performance. Low scores may be evidence of substandard performance, although many of the plans with poor results argue that they are inaccurate and were caused by reporting and data base problems. They maintain that they actually provided many more services than their scores indicated. But the NCQA believes that the numbers are telling. For one thing, if a plan cannot monitor its provision of services well, improving them becomes a difficult proposition. And in many cases, the poor numbers may well reflect an equally poor performance.

The second column shows the percentage of a plan's juvenile members who have received immunizations in a timely manner. The national average is 65.3 percent.

The third lists plans' rates of timely breast cancer screening. Breast cancer screening is one of several early detection tests that can pick up serious illnesses before they progress to critical stages. On average, 70.5 percent of adult women in HMOs receive these tests at appropriate intervals.

The next column measures the rates by which members of different plans were prescribed relatively low-cost drugs called beta blockers after heart attacks or other serious cardiac episodes. Beta blockers can trigger serious side effects, but have been proven to greatly reduce the risk of future heart attacks and cardiac death. Among those for whom beta blockers would not cause serious problems, the NCQA measured a prescription rate of only 61.9 percent, mostly because many doctors are unaware of the effectiveness of the drugs. If the managed care industry reached a prescription rate of 85 percent, the agency projects that 1,600 cardiac deaths would be avoided every year.

The fifth column measures the percentage of adult diabetic plan members who received eye examinations in 1996. Diabetes is the leading cause of adult blindness in the United States. One study estimates that regular exams could reduce blindness among diabetics by 56 percent by opening the way for laser surgery. The NCQA found that only 38.4 percent of plan members over the age of thirty received the test in the measured year. The result is not quite as dismal as it seems— only 11 percent of the diabetics in fee-for-service plans were estimated to have received the tests and many diabetics can be screened less frequently than every year. Still, the NCQA would like to see plans reach a rate of 75 percent.

The last column focuses on the average length of hospital maternity stays in different plans. So-called "drive through deliveries," in which plans covered only one day or less of a

APPENDIX A

maternity stay, generated some of the strongest criticism of the HMO industry and led to widespread changes in state laws mandating at least forty-eight hours of coverage. The average maternity stay measured by NCQA was 2.15 days.

| CHART 1 |

PLAN NAME	ACCREDITATION STATUS
Arizona	
Arizona Physicians IPA	Full
CIGNA H.C. of AZ, Private Practice Plan: Phoenix	Full
CIGNA H.C. of AZ, Staff Model: Phoenix	Full
CIGNA H.C. of AZ: Tucson	Full
Health Choice Arizona: Tempe	1 yr
HealthPartners Health Plan: Phoenix	Full
HealthPartners Health Plan: Tucson	1 yr
Intergroup of AZ: Tucson	Full
PacifiCare of AZ: Phoenix	Full
Phoenix Health Plan: Phoenix	1 yr
SCHN/MERCY CARE PLAN: Phoenix	1 yr
Arkansas	
Prudential HealthCare, Arkansas	Full
California	
Aetna US Healthcare, No.: San Bruno	Full
Aetna US Healthcare, So.: Loma Linda	Full
Aetna US Healthcare: San Diego	Full
Blue Shield of CA HMO: San Francisco	1 yr
CaliforniaCare: Woodland Hills	Full
CareAmerica Health Plans: Woodland Hills	Full
CIGNA HealthCare of No. CA: Oakland	Full
CIGNA HealthCare of San Diego	Full

APPENDIX A

PLAN NAME	ACCREDITATION STATUS
CIGNA HealthCare of So. CA: Glendale	Full
FHP, CA: Cerritos	Expired
Foundation Health: Rancho Cordova	Expired
HealthNet: Van Nuys	1 yr
Health Plan of the Redwoods: Santa Rosa	1 yr
Kaiser Foundation HP, No.CA: Oakland	1 yr
Kaiser Foundation, So. CA: Pasadena	Full
Lifeguard: San Jose	1 yr
PacifiCare of CA: Cypress	Full
Prudential HC of CA, So. Division: Woodland Hills	Full
Prudential Health Care, No. CA: San Francisco	Full
United HealthCare of CA: Long Beach	1 yr
United Health Plan: Inglewood	Denial

Colorado

CIGNA HealthCare of CO: Denver	Full
HMO Colorado: Denver	Expired
Kaiser Foundation HP of CO: Denver	Full
PacifiCare of CO: Aurora	Full
Prudential HealthCare, CO: Denver	Full
Rocky Mountain HMO: Grand Junction	1 yr

Connecticut

Aetna US Healthcare: Middletown	1 yr
Anthem Blue Cross & Blue Shield of CT: No. Haven	Full
CIGNA HealthCare of CT: Hartford	Full
ConnectiCare: Farmington	Full
Kaiser Permanente, NE region: Farmington	Full
Oxford Health Plan: Darien	On Review
Medspan and MedSpan Health Options: Hartford	Prov
Physicians Health Services: Shelton	1 yr
Prudential HealthCare	Full

APPENDIX A

CHART 1 (continued)

PLAN NAME	ACCREDITATION STATUS
Delaware	
Amerihealth HMO: Wilmington	Full
Blue Cross/Blue Shield of Delaware: Wilmington	Denial
CIGNA HealthCare of NJ;CIGNA of PA: Wilmington	Expired (1)
Principal Health Care of DE: Wilmington	1 yr
Prudential HealthCare	Full
District of Columbia	
George Washington University Health Plan	1 yr
Florida	
Aetna US Healthcare, FL: Orlando	Full
Anthem Health Plan of FL: Jacksonville	1 yr
AvMed Health Plan: Tampa/Orlando	Full
AvMed Health Plan: Gainesville	Full
AvMed Health Plan: Miami	Full
AvMed Health Plan: Fort Lauderdale	Full
AvMed Health Plan: Jacksonville	Full
Capital Health Plan: Tallahassee	Full
CIGNA HealthCare: Tampa	Full
Florida First Health Plan: Winter Haven	Prov
Foundation Health: Miami	1 yr
Health Options: Orlando	Full
Health Options; Jacksonville	Full
Health Options: Miami	Full
Health Options: Pensacola	Full
Health Options: Tampa	Full
HealthPlan SE: Tallahassee	1 yr
HIP Health Plan of FL: Fort Lauderdale	Full
Humana Medical Plan, So. Florida: Miramar	Full

APPENDIX A

PLAN NAME	ACCREDITATION STATUS
Humana Medical Plan, NE Florida: Ormond Beach	Full
Humana Medical Plan, Central Florida: Maitland	Full
Humana Medical Plan, Tampa Bay: Tampa	Full
Neighborhood Health Partnership: Miami	Full
PCA Health Plans of FL, Central region: Orlando	Full
PCA Health Plans of FL, No. region: Jacksonville	Full
PCA Health Plans of FL, So. region: Miami	Full
Principal Health Care of FL: Jacksonville	1 yr
Principal Health Care of FL: Pensacola	1 yr
Prudential HealthCare, Central FL: Maitland	Full
Prudential HealthCare: Jacksonville	Full
Prudential HealthCare, So. FL: Fort Lauderdale	Full
Prudential HealthCare of Tampa Bay: Tampa Bay	1 yr
United Health Care of FL: Miami	Expired
Georgia	
CIGNA HealthCare of GA: Atlanta	Full
HMO Georgia/BlueChoice: Atlanta	Full
Kaiser Foundation HP of GA: Atlanta	Full
Prudential HealthCare of GA: Atlanta	Full
United Health Care of GA: Atlanta	Full
Hawaii	
Blue Cross/Blue Shield of Hawaii: Honolulu	Denial
Kaiser Foundation HP of Hawaii: Honolulu	Full
Illinois	
Aetna US Healthcare of IL: Chicago	Full
BlueChoice M. C. Network Preferred: Chicago	Full
CIGNA HealthCare of IL: Des Plaines	1 yr
Health Alliance Medical Plans: Urbana	Full
Heritage National Health Plan: Moline	Prov

APPENDIX A

| CHART 1 (continued) |

PLAN NAME	ACCREDITATION STATUS
Humana Health Plan: Chicago	Full
NYLCare H.P. of the Midwest: Oakbrook Terrace	1 yr
RUSH Prudential Health Plans: Chicago	Full
Indiana	
Arnett Health Plans: Lafayette	1 yr.
M-Plan: Indianapolis	1 yr
Maxicare IN: Indianapolis	Denial
Prudential HealthCare of IN: Indianapolis	Full
United Physicians Health Network: Evansville	1 yr
Wellborn Health Plans: Evansville	1 yr
Iowa	
Medical Associates Health Plan: Dubuque	1 yr
Principal Health Care of IA; West Des Moines	1 yr
Kansas	
CIGNA HealthCare of KS/MO: Overland Park	1 yr
Kaiser Foundation HP of Kansas City: Overland Park	Full
Principal Health Care of KS: Wichita	1 yr
Kentucky	
Alternative Health Delivery Systems: Louisville	1 yr
Advantage Care: Lexington	Full
Louisiana	
Aetna U.S. Healthcare	1 yr
Gulf South Health Plans: Baton Rouge	Full
Ochsner Health Plan: Metarie	Expired
Principal Health Care of LA: Metarie	1 yr
United Health Network of LA: Baton Rouge	Expired
Maine	
Blue Cross/Blue Shield of ME: So. Portland	Full
Healthsource Maine: Freeport	Full

APPENDIX A

PLAN NAME	ACCREDITATION STATUS
Maryland	
Care First/Free State/Potomac Health Plans: Balt.	1 yr
CIGNA HealthCare Mid-Atlantic: Columbia	Full
Columbia Medical Plan: Columbia	Full
Kaiser Foundation HP of the Mid-Atlantic: Rockville	Full
Mid-Atlantic Medical Services: Rockville	1 yr
NYLCare Health Plans of Mid-Atlantic: Greenbelt	Full
Prudential HealthCare Mid-Atlantic: Balt./Wash	Prov
United HealthCare of Mid-Atlantic: Balt.	1 yr
Massachusetts	
Aetna US Healthcare, MA: Burlington	Full
Blue Cross/Blue Shield of MA: Boston	1 yr
CIGNA HealthCare of MA: Framingham	Full
Fallon Community Health Plan: Worcester	1 yr
Harvard Pilgrim Health Plan: Brookline	Full
Health New England: Springfield	Prov
Healthsource MA: Worcester	1 yr
Tufts Health Plan: Waltham	Full
Michigan	
Blue Care Network, Great Lakes: Grand Rapids	Full
Blue Care Network, East MI: Saginaw	1 yr
Blue Care Network, Mid MI: Lansing	Full
Blue Care Network, SE MI: Southfield	Full
Care Choices HMO: Farmington Hills	1 yr
Health Alliance Plans of MI: Detroit	Full
HealthPlus of MI: Flint	Full
M-Care: Ann Arbor	1 yr
OmniCare: Detroit	1 yr
Priority Health: Grand Rapids	Full
Select Care HMO: Troy	Full

APPENDIX A

| CHART 1 (continued) |

PLAN NAME	ACCREDITATION STATUS
Minnesota	
Central MN Group Health Plan: St. Cloud	Full
HealthPartners: Minneapolis	Full
Medica: Minneapolis	Full
Missouri	
Blue Cross & Blue Shield of Kansas City: KC	Full
CIGNA HealthCare of St. Louis: Clayton	Full
Group Health Plan: St. Louis	1 yr
Humana Health Plan: Kansas City	Full
Principal Health Care: Kansas City	1 yr
Prudential HealthCare: Kansas City	Full
Prudential: St. Louis	1 yr
Nebraska	
Exclusive HC:NE (Omaha)	1 yr
Principal Health Care of Nebraska: Omaha	Prov
United Healthcare of the Midlands	Full
Nevada	
Health Plan of Nevada: Las Vegas	1 yr
PacifiCare of Nevada: Las Vegas	Full
New Hampshire	
Healthsource NH: Concord	Full
Matthew Thornton Health Plan: Bedford	1 yr
New Jersey	
Aetna US Healthcare: Mt. Laurel	Full
Aetna US Healthcare: Northern NJ	Full
AmeriHealth HMO: Mt. Laurel	1 yr
CIGNA HC of No. NJ, Also d/b/a CoMed: Rockaway	Full

APPENDIX A

PLAN NAME	ACCREDITATION STATUS
HIP Health Plan of NJ: Somerset	1 yr
MediGroup of NJ, d/b/a HMO Blue: Newark	1 yr
Prudential Healthcare	Full
New Mexico	
Lovelace Health Systems: Albuquerque	Full
New York	
Capital District Physicians' Health Plan: Albany	Full
CIGNA HealthCare: Great Neck	Expired
Community Blue: Buffalo	Full
Community Health Plan: Latham	Full
Empire BlueCross/BlueShield: New York	1 yr
Finger Lakes BlueCross/BlueShield HMO: Rochester	Full
Health Care Plan: Buffalo	Full
Health Services Medi.Corp. Cent.NY: Baldwinsville	Expired
Healthsource HMO NY: Syracuse	Full
HIP of Greater NY: NY	Full
HMO CNY (BC/BS of Cent. NY): Syracuse	1 yr
Independent Health, Hudson Valley: Tarrytown	Denial
Independent Health Assoc., W NY: Buffalo	Full
MVP Health Plan: Schenectady	Full
NYLCare Health Plan of NY: Jackson Heights	1 yr
Preferred Care: Rochester	Full
Prudential Healthcare	Full
USHC NY, d/b/a Aetna US Healthcare: Uniondale	Full
WellCare of NY: Kingston	1 yr
North Carolina	
BC & BS of NC and Personal Care Plan: Durham	Full
CIGNA HealthCare of NC: Charlotte	Full
Healthsource NC: Morrisville	Full

APPENDIX A

| CHART 1 (continued) |

PLAN NAME	ACCREDITATION STATUS
Kaiser Foundation HP of NC: Raleigh	1 yr
Partners National HP of NC: Winston-Salem	Full
Prudential HealthCare System: Charlotte	1 yr
Ohio	
Aetna US Healthcare: Cleveland	Full
Anthem Blue Cross & Blue Shield: Mason	Full
AultCare: Canton	Denial
ChoiceCare: Cincinnati	Full
CIGNA HealthCare of Ohio: Cincinnati	1 yr
CIGNA HealthCare of Ohio: Columbus	1 yr
CIGNA HealthCare of Ohio, NE Div.: Cleveland	Full
Health Power HMO: Columbus	1 yr
HealthOhio-d/b/a HealthFirst: Marion	Full
The HP of the Upper Ohio Valley: St. Clairesville	Full
Humana Health Plan Ohio: Cincinnati	1 yr
Kaiser Foundation HP of Ohio: Cleveland	Full
Medical Value Plan of Health Alliance Plan: Toledo	Full
Nationwide Health Plans: Worthington	Full
Paramount HealthCare: Toledo	Full
Personal Physician Care: Cleveland	1 yr
Prudential HealthCare, No. Ohio: Cleveland	Full
Prudential HealthCare, SW Ohio/No. KY: Cincinnati	Full
Prudential HealthCare of Cent. Ohio: Columbus	1 yr
United HealthCare of Ohio, E Region: Columbus	Full
United HealthCare of Ohio, W region: Dayton	1 yr
Oklahoma	
BlueLincs HMO of OK: Tulsa	Full
CIGNA HealthCare of OK: Oklahoma City	Full

APPENDIX A

PLAN NAME	ACCREDITATION STATUS
PacifiCare of OK: Tulsa	Full
Prudential HealthCare Systems of Tulsa: Tulsa	Full
Prudential HealthCare: Oklahoma City	Full
Oregon	
Blue Cross & Blue Shield of OR, HMO OR: Portland	Full
Kaiser Foundation of the NW: Portland	Full
PacifiCare of Oregon: Lake Oswego	1 yr
QualMed Oregon Health Plan: Portland	Denial
Pennsylvania	
Aetna US Healthcare, So. NJ/Delaware: Wayne	Full
Alliance Health Network: Erie	Prov
First Priority Health/BC of NE PA: Wilkes-Barre	1 yr
Gateway Health Plan: Pittsburgh	Full
HealthAmerica of PA, E Region: Harrisburg	1 yr
HealthAmerica of W PA: Pittsburg	Full
Healthcare Management Alternatives: Philadelphia	Prov
HealthGuard of Lancaster: Lancaster	Prov
HealthPartners of Philadelphia: Philadelphia	Prov
Keystone Health Plan Central: Camp Hill	Full
Keystone Health Plan East: Philadelphia	Full
Keystone Health Plan West: Pittsburgh	1 yr
Keystone Mercy HP & AmeriHealth Mercy HP: Phila	Expired
PennState Geisinger: Danville	Full
Prudential HealthCare	Full
QualMed Plans for Health: Philadelphia	1 yr
USHC PA, d/b/a Aetna US Healthcare: Pittsburgh	Full
USHC PA, d/b/a Aetna US Healthcare: Blue Bell	Full
Rhode Island	
Coord. Health Partners, d/b/a BlueCHiP: Providence	1 yr
United HealthCare of NE: Warwick	Full

APPENDIX A

| CHART 1 (continued) |

PLAN NAME	ACCREDITATION STATUS
South Carolina	
Companion HealthCare: Columbia	Full
Healthsource So. Carolina: Charleston	1 yr
Tennessee	
CIGNA HealthCare of TN: Nashville	Full
CIGNA HealthCare of TN: Memphis	Full
Healthsource TN: Knoxville	1 yr
Medical Care Management Co.: Nashville	Denial
Prudential HealthCare Systems: Nashville	Full
Prudential HealthCare: Memphis	Full
Southern Health Plan: Memphis	1 yr
Texas	
Aetna US Healthcare: Houston	Full
Aetna US Healthcare of No. TX: Dallas	Full
CIGNA HealthCare, No. TX Div.: Irving	Full
CIGNA HealthCare, So. TX Div.: Houston	1 yr
Harris Methodist TX Health Plan: Arlington	Full
Humana HP of TX: San Ant./Houston/Dallas/Austin	Full
Kaiser Foundation HP of TX: Dallas	Full
NYLCare of the Gulf Coast: Houston	Full
NYLCare of the Southwest: Irving	Full
PCA Health Plans of TX: Austin	Full
Prudential HC: Houston/C. Christi/Rio Grande Val	Full
Prudential HealthCare System of No. TX: Dallas	Full
Prudential HealthCare Systems: San Antonio	Full
Prudential HealthCare: Austin	Full
Scott and White HP: Temple	1 yr

APPENDIX A

PLAN NAME	ACCREDITATION STATUS
Utah	
CIGNA HealthCare of UT: Salt Lake City	Full
IHC Health Plans: Salt Lake City	Full
PacifiCare of Utah: Salt Lake City	Expired
Virginia	
Aetna Health Plans of Mid-Atlantic: Falls Church	Full
CIGNA HealthCare of VA: Glen Allen	Full
HMO Virginia/Healthkeepers: Richmond	1 yr
Prudential HealthCare: Richmond	Full
Sentara Health Management: Virginia Beach	Full
Southern Health Services: Richmond	1 yr
Washington	
Group Health Cooperative of Puget Sound: Seattle	Full
Group Health Northwest: Spokane	Full
Health Plus (BC of WA & Alaska): Mountlake Ter.	Full
Medical Services Corp of E. WA: Spokane	Full
Providence Health Plans: Seattle	Denial
QualMed Washington Health Plan: Bellevue	1 yr
QualMed, Inland NW Div.: Spokane	1 yr
Wisconsin	
CareNetwork: Milwaukee	Denial
Emphesys WI Insurance: Green Bay	Denial
Family Health Plans Cooperative: Milwaukee	Denial (under review)
Group Health Cooperative So. Cent. WI: Madison	Full
PrimeCare Health Plan: Milwaukee	Full
United Health of WI: Appleton	Full

CHART 2

PLAN NAME	CHILDHOOD IMMUNIZATION	BREAST CANCER TEST	HEART MEDICATION	DIABETIC EYE EXAMS	HOSPITAL MATERNITY STAY
Arizona					
Aetna U.S. Healthcare—Arizona	NAV	72.4	NAV	47.8	1.7
CIGNA HealthCare of Arizona (Staff Model)	74	77.6	67.1	44.8	1.7
CIGNA HealthCare of Arizona (Private Practice Plan)	68.9	73.1	70.7	34.5	1.8
CIGNA HealthCare of Arizona—Tucson	56.2	71.3	NAV	50.1	2
HealthPartners Health Plans—Tucson	63.6	75.7	86.5	32.4	1.7
HMO Arizona BlueChoice	NAV	68.4	66.7	NAV	1.9
Humana Health Plan—Arizona	45.7	67.2	NAV	37.6	NAV
Intergroup of Arizona	64.3	77.8	39.6	42.7	1.9
Arkansas					
Prudential HealthCare—Arkansas (HMO)	59	66.8	NAV	17.5	1.7
Prudential HealthCare—Arkansas (POS)	59.4	73.7	NAV	25.5	1.8
California					
Aetna Health Plans of California—Loma Linda	59	63.9	NAV	35.9	NAV
Aetna Health Plans of California—San Diego	73.3	70.5	NAV	37.9	NAV

continued

PLAN NAME	CHILDHOOD IMMUNIZATION	BREAST CANCER TEST	HEART MEDICATION	DIABETIC EYE EXAMS	HOSPITAL MATERNITY STAY
Aetna U.S. Healthcare—California North	71	75	NAV	47.6	NAV
CIGNA HealthCare of Northern California—San Francisco	72.3	71.5	64.5	31	1.7
CIGNA HealthCare of San Diego	58.4	66.7	80	29.1	2.3
CIGNA Private Practice—Los Angeles IPA	51.5	65.4	51.7	29.8	NAV
Foundation Health	NAV	NAV	NAV	NAV	1.6
Health Net	61.5	70.2	65.1	41.9	1.9
Kaiser Foundation Health Plan—Northern California	77.6	75.4	82.5	53.6	1.8
Kaiser Foundation Health Plan—Southern California	63.5	77.4	84.4	58.4	1.8
Prudential Health Care Plan of California (HMO)	NAV	NAV	NAV	NAV	1.7
Prudential Health Care Plan of California (POS)	NAV	NAV	NAV	NAV	1.8
Colorado					
Antero Healthplans	53	73	28.9	43.3	1.6
CIGNA HealthCare of Denver	53	71.8	56.8	30.3	1.9
HMO Colorado	45.7	66	57.6	25.1	2.1
Kaiser Foundation Health Plan of Colorado	83.5	80.8	70.9	64.8	1.9
Prudential Health Care—Colorado (HMO)	55.8	64	NAV	37.5	2

continued

CHART 2 (continued)

PLAN NAME	CHILDHOOD IMMUNIZATION	BREAST CANCER TEST	HEART MEDICATION	DIABETIC EYE EXAMS	HOSPITAL MATERNITY STAY
Prudential Health Care—Colorado (POS)	64.3	69.3	NAV	37.4	1.9
QualMed Plans for Health of Colorado	47.8	66.7	NAV	28.6	2
San Luis Valley HMO	NAV	60.4	NAV	24	1.8
Connecticut					
Anthem Blue Cross/Blue Shield of Connecticut	81.8	77.6	83	58.2	2.5
CIGNA HealthCare of Connecticut	85.9	63.4	76.9	27.6	2.9
ConnectiCare	85.2	76.2	97.7	45	2.4
M.D. Health Plan (HMO)	91.8	69.5	NAV	52.1	2.1
M.D. Health Plan (POS)	78	67.5	NAV	43.9	2.2
Delaware					
Aetna U.S. Healthcare—Delaware	58.4	71.1	NAV	34.2	3.9
AmeriHealth HMO Delaware	59	66.4	NAV	43.5	2.3
CIGNA HealthCare of Delaware—Wilmington	42.9	72	NAV	13.5	2.2
Principal Health Care of Delaware	59.6	71.7	46.6	37.7	1.9
Florida					
Aetna U.S. Healthcare—Tampa	68.3	65.6	NAV	31.2	2.2
AvMed Health Plan—Ft. Lauderdale area	NAV	71.7	NAV	47.4	1.8

continued

PLAN NAME	CHILDHOOD IMMUNIZATION	BREAST CANCER TEST	HEART MEDICATION	DIABETIC EYE EXAMS	HOSPITAL MATERNITY STAY
AvMed Health Plan—Gainesville area	NAV	73.5	NAV	52.3	2.1
AvMed Health Plan—Jacksonville area	NAV	73	NAV	40.5	1.9
AvMed Health Plan—Miami area	NAV	71.2	63.3	41.8	1.8
AvMed Health Plan—Orlando area	NAV	74	NAV	30.7	1.8
AvMed Health Plan—Tampa area	NAV	71.6	NAV	43.5	1.9
CIGNA HealthCare of Florida—Jacksonville	64.3	66	NAV	29.1	2
CIGNA HealthCare of Florida—Orlando	52.3	71.1	59.4	24.3	1.5
CIGNA HealthCare of Florida—Tampa	65.2	72.1	73.6	48.7	2
CIGNA HealthCare of South Florida	64.7	65.2	68.8	27	1.8
Foundation Health—Florida	73	64	44.1	17.1	1.5
Health Options of Florida	44.5	70.5	71.5	35.8	2.1
HIP Health Plan of Florida	81.8	70.8	58.8	44	2.1
Humana Health Plan—Central Florida	51.5	68.3	NAV	54.7	NAV
Humana Health Plan—Tampa	65.8	70	79.5	51.3	NAV
Neighborhood Health Partnership	NAV	70.5	NAV	NAV	1.9
PCA Health Plans of Florida—Central	62.5	65.7	NAV	27.8	NAV
PCA Health Plans of Florida—North	63.3	71.5	NAV	25.6	NAV

continued

CHART 2 (continued)

PLAN NAME	CHILDHOOD IMMUNIZATION	BREAST CANCER TEST	HEART MEDICATION	DIABETIC EYE EXAMS	HOSPITAL MATERNITY STAY
PCA Health Plans of Florida—South	78	68.9	44.7	8.7	NAV
Prudential Health Care—Central Florida (HMO)	78.1	80.8	79.2	42.8	1.9
Prudential Health Care—Central Florida (POS)	58.8	73.5	NAV	25.3	1.9
Prudential Health Care—Jacksonville (HMO)	73.9	74	74.3	56.2	2.1
Prudential Health Care—Jacksonville (POS)	78	68.4	NAV	44.4	2.1
Prudential Health Care—South Florida (HMO)	62.3	65	82	12.7	2.1
Prudential Health Care—South Florida (POS)	67.5	67.9	NAV	21.7	2
Prudential Health Care—Tampa Bay (HMO)	NAV	78.8	66.7	NAV	2.1
Prudential Health Care—Tampa Bay (POS)	NAV	73.7	NAV	NAV	2
Georgia					
Aetna U.S. Healthcare—Georgia (HMO)	NAV	NAV	NAV	25	2.9
Aetna U.S. Healthcare—Georgia (POS)	NAV	NAV	NAV	20.5	2.6
CIGNA HealthCare of Georgia—Atlanta	58.6	59.1	39	20.7	2.4
Kaiser Foundation Health Plan of Georgia	70.2	73.8	66.2	41	2.1
Prudential Health Care—Atlanta (HMO)	55	70.6	68.3	28	2.2
Prudential Health Care—Atlanta (POS)	70.1	75.7	62.9	33.6	2.2

continued

PLAN NAME	CHILDHOOD IMMUNIZATION	BREAST CANCER TEST	HEART MEDICATION	DIABETIC EYE EXAMS	HOSPITAL MATERNITY STAY
Hawaii					
Kaiser Foundation Health Plan—Hawaii	78.6	77.7	83.3	67.4	2.3
Illinois					
Aetna U.S. Healthcare—Illinois	67.2	64.3	NAV	43.4	1.9
American HMO Illinois/Indiana (HMO)	NAV	NAV	NAV	NAV	NAV
American HMO Illinois/Indiana (POS)	NAV	NAV	NAV	NAV	2
CIGNA HealthCare of Illinois—Chicago	55	58.6	27.5	16.4	1.8
Health Alliance Medical Plans	84.7	83.1	NAV	42.6	1.8
Humana Health Plan—Chicago	56.6	68.4	84.4	43.3	NAV
PersonalCare Insurance of Illinois	74.9	70.4	NAV	22.9	2.2
Rush Prudential Health Plans (HMO)	66.9	67.9	83	25.8	2.2
Rush Prudential Health Plans (POS)	65.7	64.2	NAV	19.2	2
Indiana					
Healthsource Indiana	72	65.6	NAV	23.8	1.8
M-Care	82.6	77.5	64.5	37.1	2
Partners Health Plan of Indiana	49.9	NAV	NAV	NAV	2.1
Prudential Health Care—Indiana (HMO)	59.5	76.1	NAV	33.5	1.9

continued

CHART 2 (continued)

PLAN NAME	CHILDHOOD IMMUNIZATION	BREAST CANCER TEST	HEART MEDICATION	DIABETIC EYE EXAMS	HOSPITAL MATERNITY STAY
Prudential Health Care—Indiana (POS)	69.2	70.8	NAV	33	1.9
Welborn Health Plans	76.3	87.8	NAV	59.4	2.3
Iowa					
Unity Choice Health Plan	62.6	78.2	NAV	47	2.3
KANSAS					
Preferred Plus of Kansas	55.8	66.5	NAV	NAV	1.9
Prudential Health Care—Topeka	NAV	80.3	NAV	47.6	2.1
Kentucky					
Humana Health Plan—Lexington	76.7	67.5	NAV	46	NAV
Humana Health Plan (Louisville)	63	62.9	NAV	46	NAV
Humana Health Plan (Louisville-KPPA)	64.1	63.9	NAV	38	NAV
Louisiana					
Aetna U.S. Healthcare—Louisiana	NAV	61.8	NAV	26	2
CIGNA HealthCare of Louisiana—Baton Rouge	37.2	69.6	NAV	20.7	1.9
CIGNA HealthCare of Northern Louisiana—Shreveport	22.4	66.3	NAV	28.8	1.7
Gulf South Health Plans	61	68.6	NAV	38.5	1.8

continued

PLAN NAME	CHILDHOOD IMMUNIZATION	BREAST CANCER TEST	HEART MEDICATION	DIABETIC EYE EXAMS	HOSPITAL MATERNITY STAY
Massachusetts					
Aetna U.S. Healthcare—Massachusetts (HMO)	NAV	75.1	NAV	NAV	3.3
Aetna U.S. Healthcare—Massachusetts (POS)	NAV	75.1	NAV	NAV	3
CIGNA HealthCare of Massachusetts—Springfield	81.3	71.5	NAV	51.6	3
Fallon Community Health Plan	92.5	84.2	87.9	62	2.4
Harvard Community Health Plan	87.6	81.3	90.7	66.3	2.7
Health New England	75.5	76.1	NAV	54	2.1
Healthsource Massachusetts	87.3	78.1	91.1	26	2.6
HMO Blue—Boston	92.9	81	89.5	58.6	2.8
Neighborhood Health Plan	87.4	72	NAV	53.8	2.7
Pilgrim Health Care	83.7	83	87.4	49.4	2.8
Tufts Health Plan	88.8	76.2	97.9	51.6	2.7
Maine					
Blue Cross and Blue Shield of Maine (HMO)	73.1	80.7	NAV	52.9	2.6
Blue Cross and Blue Shield of Maine (POS)	76.2	84.7	100	57.4	2.6
Healthsource Maine	79.6	84.4	NAV	57.8	2.3

continued

CHART 2 (continued)

PLAN NAME	CHILDHOOD IMMUNIZATION	BREAST CANCER TEST	HEART MEDICATION	DIABETIC EYE EXAMS	HOSPITAL MATERNITY STAY
Maryland					
Aetna Health Plans of the Mid-Atlantic	60.3	58.6	NAV	34.7	2.1
Aetna U.S. Healthcare—Maryland (HMO)	NAV	59.5	NAV	34.6	2.7
Aetna U.S. Healthcare—Maryland (POS)	NAV	65.9	NAV	26.6	2.9
CFS Health Group (HMO—IPA)	74.5	70.6	80.8	38.8	2.1
CFS Health Group (HMO—Group)	63.8	70.1	86.5	35.1	2.2
CIGNA HealthCare of the Mid-Atlantic	55.5	57.2	35.3	33.6	2.4
Columbia Medical Plan (HMO)	91	83.7	NAV	56	1.8
Columbia Medical Plan (POS)	89.8	83.1	NAV	63.3	1.8
Delmarva Health Plan (HMO)	66.7	77.3	NAV	NAV	2
Delmarva Health Plan (POS)	58.7	77.2	NAV	NAV	2.1
Kaiser Foundation Health Plan of the Mid-Atlantic States	72	77.1	64.2	58.3	2.1
Mid Atlantic Medical Services	72.3	69.2	42.3	32.4	2.1
NYLCare of the Mid-Atlantic	82.2	70.8	71.6	49.9	2
PHN-HMO	65.8	70.8	NAV	33.8	2.2

continued

PLAN NAME	CHILDHOOD IMMUNIZATION	BREAST CANCER TEST	HEART MEDICATION	DIABETIC EYE EXAMS	HOSPITAL MATERNITY STAY
Prudential Health Care of the Mid-Atlantic (HMO)	69.1	61.6	65	50.1	2
Prudential Health Care of the Mid-Atlantic (POS)	79	67.6	NAV	44	2
Michigan					
Blue Care Network—Great Lakes	71	79.3	57	31.4	1.9
Blue Care Network—Eastern Michigan	57.7	85.2	NAV	68.1	2
Blue Care Network—Mid-Michigan	66.2	83	NAV	34.5	2
Blue Care Network—Southeast Michigan	61.6	66.9	28.6	30.1	2.2
Blue Choice (HMO)	54.7	66.2	NAV	28.4	1.7
Blue Choice (POS)	48.6	58.4	NAV	22.1	1.6
Care Choices HMO/Mercy Health Plans	40.5	78.6	63.8	39.1	2.1
Health Alliance Plan of Michigan	72.4	72.4	63	47.5	1.8
HealthPlus of Michigan	78.8	84.7	57.4	60.3	2.1
M Plan	65.9	77.9	75.5	42.8	1.9
NorthMed	84.2	74.3	NAV	40.4	2.2
Priority Health—Michigan (HMO)	NAV	82.2	53.1	21.9	2
Priority Health—Michigan (POS)	19.1	73.9	NAV	15.8	2.3
SelectCare HMO	65.9	71.3	57.1	37.2	2.2

continued

CHART 2 (continued)

PLAN NAME	CHILDHOOD IMMUNIZATION	BREAST CANCER TEST	HEART MEDICATION	DIABETIC EYE EXAMS	HOSPITAL MATERNITY STAY
Minnesota					
Central Minnesota Group Health Plan	63.3	88.2	NAV	76.5	2.6
HealthPartners	71.6	77.6	80.1	50.6	2.5
Missouri					
CIGNA HealthCare of St. Louis	20.9	51.9	NAV	20.4	1.8
CIGNA HealthCare of Kansas City	60.3	68.1	40	12.9	1.9
Exclusive Healthcare—Kansas City (HMO)	49.2	68.2	NAV	25.6	NAV
Exclusive Healthcare—Kansas City (POS)	NAV	NAV	NAV	NAV	1.8
Group Health Plan—St. Louis (HMO)	70.1	81.5	78.1	38.2	2.3
Group Health Plan—St. Louis (POS)	64.1	75.2	NAV	37.2	2.5
Humana Health Plan—Kansas City	69	73.2	58.1	67.2	NAV
Kaiser Foundation Health Plan of Kansas City	82.8	75.4	NAV	59.7	1.9
Principal Health Care of Kansas City	75.4	79.9	NAV	30	1.8
Prudential Health Care—Kansas City (HMO)	64.1	71.8	NAV	45.1	1.9
Prudential Health Care—Kansas City (POS)	67.1	75.7	NAV	44.8	1.8

continued

PLAN NAME	CHILDHOOD IMMUNIZATION	BREAST CANCER TEST	HEART MEDICATION	DIABETIC EYE EXAMS	HOSPITAL MATERNITY STAY
Prudential Health Care—St. Louis (HMO)	70	70.6	NAV	28.2	1.8
Prudential Health Care—St. Louis (POS)	71	67.4	35.6	32.1	1.9
Nebraska					
Exclusive Health Care—Omaha (HMO)	71.8	71	48.5	20.4	2
Exclusive Healthcare—Omaha (POS)	NAV	NAV	NAV	8.2	NAV
HMO Nebraska (HMO)	57.7	76.8	NAV	19.7	1.9
HMO Nebraska (POS)	57.7	73.9	NAV	11.1	1.9
Nevada					
Exclusive Health Care—Nevada	31.5	61.9	NAV	8.2	2.1
New Hampshire					
Blue Choice	62	75.2	NAV	52.3	2.2
Healthsource New Hampshire	93	74.8	81	53	2.2
Matthew Thornton Health Plan	84.4	83.7	57.1	76.9	2.2
New Jersey					
CIGNA HealthCare of Northern New Jersey	59.4	51.3	66.2	21.4	2.8
CIGNA HealthCare of Southern New Jersey	26.3	44.8	NAV	14.4	2.9

continued

CHART 2 (continued)

PLAN NAME	CHILDHOOD IMMUNIZATION	BREAST CANCER TEST	HEART MEDICATION	DIABETIC EYE EXAMS	HOSPITAL MATERNITY STAY
HIP Health Plan of New Jersey	78.8	71.8	64.5	54.5	2.6
HMO Blue of New Jersey	57.4	58.2	NAV	32.2	2.4
Prudential Health Care—New Jersey, New York, Connecticut (HMO)	67.1	60.3	58.6	46.5	2.7
Prudential Health Care—New Jersey, New York, Connecticut (POS)	60.8	58.2	54.8	42.9	2.7
New Mexico					
Lovelace Health Systems	77.4	75.7	66.7	53.3	3.1
Presbyterian Health Plan (HMO)	74.5	55.3	NAV	31.2	
Presbyterian Health Plan (POS)	75.2	53.7	NAV	31.4	
Presbyterian Health Plan (PPO)	NAV	62.8	NAV	NAV	
QalMed Health Plan of New Mexico	52.2	72.7	NAV	29.5	2
New York					
Aetna U.S. Healthcare—New York (HMO)	NAV	67.3	47.4	56.8	3.4
Aetna U.S. Healthcare—New York (POS)	NAV	68.2	46.5	48.4	3.6
Blue Cross/Blue Shield of Western New York—Choice Blue (POS)	90.5	76.2	NAV	36.6	2.9

continued

PLAN NAME	CHILDHOOD IMMUNIZATION	BREAST CANCER TEST	HEART MEDICATION	DIABETIC EYE EXAMS	HOSPITAL MATERNITY STAY
Blue Cross/Blue Shield of Western New York—Community Blue (HMO)	90.5	74.3	NAV	37.6	2.7
Capital District Physicians' Health Plan	86.6	71.7	64.7	51	2.6
CIGNA HealthCare of New York	50.4	51.3	NAV	16.5	3.6
Empire Blue Cross/Blue Shield Healthnet	71	66.7	40.9	32.6	2.8
Finger Lakes Health Insurance Co. (HMO)	75.4	76.8	83.4	54.2	2.7
Finger Lakes Health Insurance Co. (POS)	75.4	76.8	83.4	54.2	2.7
Health Care Plan, Inc.	90	75.2	70.6	71.3	2.4
Health Services Medical Corp. (HMO)	78.7	73.4	70.8	54.2	2.6
Health Services Medical Corp. (POS)	73.8	75.6	NAV	45.6	2.9
Healthsource HMO of New York (Patient's Choice)	86.9	81.3	NAV	40.3	2.7
HIP of Greater New York	59.1	70.3	NAV	55.7	2.9
Independent Health Metro-Hudson Region #2 (HMO)	64.2	69.2	NAV	39.2	2.8
Independent Health Metro-Hudson Region #2 (POS)	NAV	68.6	NAV	38.7	4.1
Managed Health Inc. (HMO)	NAV	77.6	NAV	52.7	NAV
Managed Health Inc. (POS)	NAV	84.5	NAV	54.1	2.5
MDNY Healthcare (HMO)	NAV	NAV	NAV	27.7	2

continued

| CHART 2 (continued) |

PLAN NAME	CHILDHOOD IMMUNIZATION	BREAST CANCER TEST	HEART MEDICATION	DIABETIC EYE EXAMS	HOSPITAL MATERNITY STAY
MVP Health Plan	81.1	68.1	76.3	37.3	3
NYLCare of the New York Region (HMO)	NAV	61.1	74.5	50.1	2.8
NYLCare of the New York Region (POS)	38.7	63.5	57.5	32.2	3.1
Rochester Are HMO, Inc. (Preferred Care)	84.9	80	63.6	45.5	2.8
North Carolina					
CIGNA HealthCare of North Carolina—Raleigh	52.8	68.4	50	24.3	2.4
Healthsource North Carolina	82.2	79.1	67.9	27.3	2.5
Kaiser Foundation Health Plan of North Carolina	NAV	NAV	NAV	54.6	2.2
Partners National Health Plans of North Carolina (HMO)	88.6	74.7	38.1	33.8	1.9
Partners National Health Plans of North Carolina (POS)	NAV	74.6	NAV	37.5	2
Personal Care Plan of North Carolina	66.7	61.4	63.2	40.2	2.5
Prudential Health Care—Charlotte (HMO)	NAV	72.5	NAV	26	2.3
Prudential Health Care—Charlotte (POS)	NAV	68	NAV	26.8	2.3
Prudential Health Care—Raleigh/Durham (HMO)	71.4	83	NAV	29.2	2.8
Prudential Health Care—Raleigh/Durham (POS)	NAV	NAV	NAV	43.3	2.5

continued

PLAN NAME	CHILDHOOD IMMUNIZATION	BREAST CANCER TEST	HEART MEDICATION	DIABETIC EYE EXAMS	HOSPITAL MATERNITY STAY
Ohio					
ChoiceCare (HMO)	57.2	77.2	48.1	29.2	1.9
ChoiceCare (POS)	58.4	77.4	38.5	25.3	1.9
CIGNA HealthCare of Cleveland	54.5	61.8	38.7	25.3	2.1
CIGNA HealthCare of Ohio—Cincinnati	68.2	49.4	NAV	27.7	1.8
CIGNA HealthCare of Ohio—Columbus	58.4	63.2	35.3	28.7	1.9
DayMed Health Maintenance Plan	65.9	59.6	NAV	37.5	NAV
Family Health Plan	26.8	58.4	NAV	13.4	NAV
Humana Health Plan of Ohio	54.2	65.3	NAV	34.9	NAV
Kaiser Foundation Health Plan of Ohio	76.9	75.9	90.5	58.9	1.9
Prudential Health Care—Central Ohio (HMO)	60.9	62.2	NAV	23.1	2.1
Prudential Health Care—Central Ohio (POS)	72.5	63.9	NAV	18	1.8
Prudential Health Care—Northern Ohio (HMO)	53.8	67.8	NAV	40.1	2
Prudential Health Care—Northern Ohio (POS)	66.2	69.6	NAV	46.5	2.1
Prudential Health Care—Southwest Ohio/ Northern Kentucky (HMO)	67.1	69.1	NAV	43.9	2

continued

CHART 2 (continued)

PLAN NAME	CHILDHOOD IMMUNIZATION	BREAST CANCER TEST	HEART MEDICATION	DIABETIC EYE EXAMS	HOSPITAL MATERNITY STAY
Prudential Health Care—Southwest Ohio/ Northern Kentucky (POS)	74.5	70.6	NAV	44.8	1.9
Oklahoma					
BlueLines HMO	53.4	72.3	NAV	28.2	1.9
CIGNA HealthCare of Oklahoma	93.9	65.1	NAV	21.2	1.8
CIGNA HealthCare of Oklahoma—Tulsa	87.8	58.2	NAV	20.2	2.1
Prudential Health Care—Oklahoma City (HMO)	71.1	79.8	52.6	46.5	1.9
Prudential Health Care—Oklahoma City (POS)	64	74	NAV	34.4	1.7
Prudential Health Care—Tulsa (HMO)	70	74.7	77.4	42.3	2.1
Prudential Health Care—Tulsa (POS)	61.3	73.2	93.5	29.7	2.1
Oregon					
HMO Oregon	40.9	73.6	78.8	28.5	1.9
Kaiser Foundation Health Plan of the Northwest	70.8	76.6	79	62.9	2.2
PACC Health Plans (HMO)	63	69.8	49.9	42.1	NAV
PACC Health Plans (POS)	63	69.8	49.9	42.1	NAV
PACC Health Plans (PPO)	63	69.8	49.9	42.1	NAV

continued

PLAN NAME	CHILDHOOD IMMUNIZATION	BREAST CANCER TEST	HEART MEDICATION	DIABETIC EYE EXAMS	HOSPITAL MATERNITY STAY
Providence Health Plan of Oregon	76.2	75.4	71.4	36.1	2
QualMed Oregon Health Plan	51.1	67.7	44.7	34.2	1.8
Pennsylvania					
Aetna U.S. Healthcare—Central Pennsylvania	NAV	77.4	NAV	30.9	3.2
Aetna U.S. Healthcare—Pittsburgh (HMO)	59.1	76.1	NAV	31.7	2.6
Aetna U.S. Healthcare—Pittsburgh (POS)	63.4	69.8	NAV	30.9	2.6
Aetna U.S. Healthcare—Southeastern Pennsylvania (HMO)	68.3	78.1	63.2	39.8	2.9
Aetna U.S. Healthcare—Southeastern Pennsylvania (POS)	65	74.4	59.2	41.6	3
CIGNA HealthCare of Pennsylvania—Philadelphia	46.7	41.4	NAV	14.8	2.3
First Priority HMO of Northeast Pennsylvania (HMO)	71.3	60.6	83.8	15.8	2.9
First Priority HMO of Northeast Pennsylvania (POS)	69.2	63	NAV	17.9	2.9
Geisinger Health Plan	61.6	76.4	40	66.4	2.1
HealthAmerica Pennsylvania—Eastern Pennsylvania (HMO)	NAV	76.9	87.9	33.3	2.3
HealthAmerica Pennsylvania—Eastern Pennsylvania (POS)	NAV	53.8	NAV	36.4	2.3
HealthAmerica Pennsylvania—Pittsburgh (HMO)	86	78.7	58.2	57.2	2.2
HealthAmerica Pennsylvania—Pittsburgh (POS)	78.6	70	NAV	42.9	2.2
HealthAmerica Pennsylvania—Pittsburgh (PPO)	NAV	NAV	NAV	NAV	2.3

continued

CHART 2 (continued)

PLAN NAME	CHILDHOOD IMMUNIZATION	BREAST CANCER TEST	HEART MEDICATION	DIABETIC EYE EXAMS	HOSPITAL MATERNITY STAY
HealthGuard of Lancaster (HMO)	61.3	76.9	NAV	38.2	2.4
HealthGuard of Lancaster (POS)	61.3	76.9	NAV	38.2	2.2
Keystone Health Plan—Central	68.9	76.5	95.1	31.8	2.3
Keystone Health Plan—East	69.8	68.4	80.7	45.7	2.5
Keystone Health Plan West—KeystoneBlue (HMO)	69.6	69.8	52.6	19	2.5
Keystone Health Plan West—SelectBlue (POS)	69.6	75.2	48.9	21.2	2.4
Prudential Health Care—Pennsylvania/Delaware (HMO)	74.5	73.2	NAV	39.8	2.2
Prudential Health Care—Pennsylvania/Delaware (POS)	76	67.4	NAV	49.1	2.2
QualMed Philadelphia Health Plan	54.8	63.8	28.6	25.4	2.6
South Carolina					
Companion HealthCare	NAV	74.6	34.9	38.2	2.3
Healthsource South Carolina	80.8	77.2	73.7	14.1	2.4
South Dakota					
Mutual of Omaha of South Dakota and Community Health (HMO)	NAV	NAV	NAV	NAV	NAV
Mutual of Omaha of South Dakota and Community Health (POS)	NAV	NAV	NAV	NAV	1.8

continued

PLAN NAME	CHILDHOOD IMMUNIZATION	BREAST CANCER TEST	HEART MEDICATION	DIABETIC EYE EXAMS	HOSPITAL MATERNITY STAY
Tennessee					
CIGNA HealthCare of Tennessee—Memphis	61.6	58.6	NAV	12.2	2
CIGNA HealthCare of Tennessee—Nashville	62.8	63.6	32.4	14.5	2
Harris Methodist Health Plan	64.2	66.9	40.6	42.7	2.5
Prudential Health Care—Memphis (HMO)	59.9	73.7	NAV	46	1.9
Prudential Health Care—Memphis (POS)	54.7	71.7	NAV	24.4	2.1
Prudential Health Care—Nashville (HMO)	53.5	66.9	NAV	41.8	1.8
Prudential Health Care—Nashville (POS)	NAV	73.7	NAV	37.5	1.8
Southern Health Plan (The Apple Plan) (HMO)	45.5	59.4	NAV	22.6	2
Southern Health Plan (The Apple Plan) (HMO)	45.5	59.4	NAV	22.6	2.4
Texas					
CIGNA HealthCare of Texas—Dallas	57.7	71.1	59.5	37.9	2.1
CIGNA HealthCare of Texas—Houston	70.1	70.3	31.3	28.5	2.1
Exclusive Healthcare—Dallas (HMO)	40.3	35	NAV	8.6	NAV
Exclusive Healthcare—Dallas (POS)	NAV	NAV	NAV	NAV	1.9
Humana Health Plan of Texas—Corpus Christi	57.1	69.2	NAV	20	NAV
Humana Health Plan of Texas—San Antonio	64.7	74.7	NAV	40.9	NAV

continued

CHART 2 (continued)

PLAN NAME	CHILDHOOD IMMUNIZATION	BREAST CANCER TEST	HEART MEDICATION	DIABETIC EYE EXAMS	HOSPITAL MATERNITY STAY
Kaiser Foundation Health Plan of Texas	81.6	67.6	70	38	1.8
NYLCare Health Plans of the Southwest	56	72	53.2	38.4	1.8
NYLCare of the Gulf Coast (HMO)	57.7	65.7	61.2	32.8	2.4
NYLCare of the Gulf Coast (POS)	53.1	67.7	64.1	18	2.2
Prudential Health Care—Amarillo	NAV	64.3	NAV	28.8	2
Prudential Health Care—Austin/Central Texas (HMO)	58.5	60.8	NAV	40	1.8
Prudential Health Care—Austin/Central Texas (POS)	65.8	66.3	NAV	36.7	1.9
Prudential Health Care—Corpus Christi	NAV	NAV	NAV	NAV	NAV
Prudential Health Care—Houston (HMO)	54.5	79.3	64.6	42.8	2
Prudential Health Care—Houston (POS)	55.7	64.7	47.1	41.6	2.1
Prudential Health Care—North Texas (HMO)	61.1	66.4	NAV	32.1	1.9
Prudential Health Care—North Texas (POS)	68.4	72	38.4	34.1	1.8
Prudential Health Care—San Antonio (HMO)	55.3	64.7	NAV	50.4	2
Prudential Health Care—San Antonio (POS)	66.7	72.7	84.8	31.6	1.9
Prudential Health Care—TAC-Beaumont, Corpus Christi (POS)	39.7	67.2	NAV	31.7	2.5
PCA Health Plans of Texas	76.3	65.3	55.3	22.9	1.7

continued

PLAN NAME	CHILDHOOD IMMUNIZATION	BREAST CANCER TEST	HEART MEDICATION	DIABETIC EYE EXAMS	HOSPITAL MATERNITY STAY
Utah					
CIGNA HealthCare of Utah—Salt Lake City	35.3	63.5	NAV	20.8	1.5
United HealthCare of Utah (HMO)	41.8	73	NAV	29.4	1.8
United HealthCare of Utah (POS)	41.8	67.1	NAV	24.5	2
Virginia					
CIGNA HealthCare of Virginia	36	66.5	31.8	21.8	2.2
Prudential Health Care—Richmond (HMO)	NAV	NAV	NAV	NAV	1.9
Prudential Health Care—Richmond (POS)	NAV	NAV	NAV	NAV	1.9
Southern Health Services	82.4	74.6	39.5	30.8	1.9
Trigon Blue Cross/Blue Shield	56.6	66	51.9	27.3	2.1
Vermont					
Kaiser Foundation Health Plan, CHP	85.2	81	81.7	59.4	2.2
Kaiser Foundation Health Plan, Northeast Region	87.8	81.4	83.3	73.7	2.1
Washington					
Group Health Cooperative of Puget Sound	89.1	71.3	85	59.6	1.7
Group Health Northwest	68.6	89	37	58.1	2
HealthPlus—Washington State	56.8	82.3	NAV	66.7	1.9

continued

CHART 2 (continued)

PLAN NAME	CHILDHOOD IMMUNIZATION	BREAST CANCER TEST	HEART MEDICATION	DIABETIC EYE EXAMS	HOSPITAL MATERNITY STAY
Medical Services Corporation of Eastern Washington	54.7	73.4	NAV	44.1	1.8
Options Health Care	68.2	71.8	NAV	47.7	1.9
QualMed Washington Health Plan—Bellevue	64.7	75.2	43.4	44.2	1.7
QualMed Washington Health Plan—Spokane	55.6	64	48.8	31.1	2
Virginia Mason—Group Health Alliance (HMO)	88.9	70.8	NAV	51.7	1.8
Virginia Mason—Group Health Alliance (POS)	67.7	63.9	NAV	65.7	1.7
Virginia Mason Health Plan	68.4	83.9	NAV	67.3	1.3
Washington, D.C.					
George Washington University Health Plan	55.5	70.8	NAV	48.8	NAV
Wisconsin					
Compcare—Wisconsin	64.8	75	31.3	49.4	1.9
Family Health Plan Cooperative	92.2	74.6	75	77.2	2.6
Group Health Cooperative of Eau Claire	68.2	82.9	NAV	41	2.1
Group Health Cooperative of South Central Wisconsin	84.4	83.5	NAV	54	2.7
Humana Medical Plan—Milwaukee	66.4	67.6	NAV	56.4	2
Network Health Plan of Wisconsin	85.9	79.3	NAV	65.5	1.7

APPENDIX B

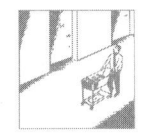

FEDERAL SURVEY

The annual survey of Federal employees is the most extensive poll undertaken nationally of consumer health plan preferences. Nearly 80,000 government workers participated in the survey in 1997, expressing a range of opinions about more than three hundred plans. The error rate for the question in the poll measuring members' overall satisfaction with their plans is less than 6 percent, meaning that if the survey were repeated, the results would likely be similar 95 percent of the time.

The first column shows the percentage of respondents who were "extremely satisfied" with their plan, the second "very satisfied," and the third "somewhat satisfied." Pay particular attention to the first column, since it registers the feelings of people who had notably good experiences. But keep in mind that most people of good health are more or less satisfied with their plans. It is the experiences of those who underwent serious medical episodes that may be truer measures of satisfaction and, as yet, these are unmeasured by the survey, which is sponsored by the Federal Office of Personnel Management.

The next four columns measure the percent of respondents who rate their plan from good to excellent on measures of great importance to consumers. The first concerns the plan's coverage package, the second the breadth of choice of doctors within the plan, the third how easy it is to get an appointment when you are sick, the fourth the quality of medical care provided. The last column indicates when a plan is one of the top-rated ones on the survey.

CHART 2—HMOS

PLAN NAME	EXTREMELY SATISFIED	VERY SATISFIED	SOMEWHAT SATISFIED	COVERAGE	CHOICE OF DOCTORS	APPOINTMENTS CASE	QUALITY	TOP RATED
Arizona								
Aetna US Healthcare: Phoenix/Tucson areas	27	37	22	89	83	76	91	
Cigna HC of AZ, Phoenix: Phoenix area	18	41	24	88	74	79	91	
HealthPartners Health Plans: Northern/Central Arizona	20	41	22	84	84	81	92	
Humana Health Plan of AZ: Phoenix/Tucson/Southern Arizona	16	36	26	78	74	74	85	
Intergroup of Arizona, Inc.: Maricopa/Pima/Other AZ counties	20	36	27	86	74	66	85	
PacifiCare of Arizona: Most of Arizona	14	38	28	84	68	69	85	
Pacificare of Nevada: Part of Mojave County	13	27	30	76	56	70	78	
Arkansas								
HEALTH ADVANTAGE: All of Arkansas								
Healthsource Arkansas: Central/Northern/Northwest Arkansas	13	43	24	81	77	79	88	
United HealthCare of Arkansas: Little Rock/Ft. Smith areas	13	42	26	86	82	79	89	
California								
Aetna US Healthcare: Southern California	16	39	23	82	79	79	89	
Blue Shield of CA Access + HMO: Most of California	13	34	28	80	70	78	85	
CaliforniaCare: Most of California	20	37	26	82	70	76	86	

continued

CHART 2—HMOS (continued)

PLAN NAME	EXTREMELY SATISFIED	VERY SATISFIED	SOMEWHAT SATISFIED	COVERAGE	CHOICE OF DOCTORS	APPOINTMENTS CASE	QUALITY	TOP RATED
CareAmerica HP:Southern California	20	37	24	83	75	77	84	
CIGNA HealthCare of CA: Northern and Southern California	16	37	29	84	76	80	85	
Foundation Health: Northern California	11	33	23	76	70	76	87	
Health Net: Most of California	17	42	26	84	77	82	88	
Kaiser Permanente: Northern California	22	46	21	91	79	83	90	
Kaiser Permanente: Southern California	25	40	22	90	78	78	87	
Maxicare Northern California: Northern California	20	32	29	85	81	88	89	
Maxicare Southern California: Southern California	18	38	27	82	76	81	85	
National HMO Health Plan: Northern/Central/Southern California	11	48	20	77	78	79	87	
Omni Healthcare: Central Valley/Sacramento/No. California	20	41	25	85	80	85	91	
PacifiCare of California: Most of California	18	34	27	85	75	70	84	
United Health Plan: LA/Orange/San Bernardino								
Colorado								
Kaiser Permanente: Denver area, Colorado Springs area	23	48	19	90	85	87	90	Yes
PacifiCare of Colorado-High: Denver/Pueblo/Col.Springs/Fort Collins	17	47	22	86	81	82	89	

continued

PLAN NAME	EXTREMELY SATISFIED	VERY SATISFIED	SOMEWHAT SATISFIED	COVERAGE	CHOICE OF DOCTORS	APPOINTMENTS CASE	QUALITY	TOP RATED
PacifiCare of Colorado, Std: Denver/Pueblo/Col.Springs/Fort Collins	12	41	27	82	76	76	88	
Rocky Mountain HMO: Most of Colorado	24	48	18	85	88	87	89	Yes
Connecticut								
Aetna US Healthcare: All of Connecticut	19	32	29	85	77	85	89	
ConnectiCare: All of Connecticut	21	47	21	87	92	93	93	
Harvard Community Health Plan: Northwest CT	25	43	20	91	87	88	92	Yes
Health New England: Northern CT	30	48	17	96	86	88	88	Yes
Kaiser Permanente: Most of CT	25	37	23	89	82	90	92	
M.D. Health Plan: All of CT	20	49	25	95	94	92	94	Yes
NYLCare Health Plans: Fairfield County	15	35	27	84	69	70	77	
Delaware								
Aetna US Healthcare: All of Delaware	16	40	29	90	70	89	88	
District of Columbia								
Aetna US Healthcare	19	36	29	86	76	79	81	
CareFirst	15	35	34	87	69	77	83	
CIGNA HealthCare Mid-Atlantic	15	34	27	86	71	77	81	

continued

CHART 2 — HMOS (continued)

PLAN NAME	EXTREMELY SATISFIED	VERY SATISFIED	SOMEWHAT SATISFIED	COVERAGE	CHOICE OF DOCTORS	APPOINTMENTS CASE	QUALITY	TOP RATED
George Washington Univ HP, High	23	42	23	92	80	83	89	
George Washington Univ HP, Std	12	40	27	88	74	74	83	
Kaiser Permanente	17	35	28	88	77	74	81	
MD-IPA	19	41	27	88	78	80	90	
NYLCare/Mid-Atlantic, High	19	39	26	91	74	82	88	
NYLCare/Mid-Atlantic, Std	11	36	32	85	72	75	80	
Florida								
Capital Health Plan: Capital Health Plan: Tallahassee area	31	50	15	94	92	87	92	Yes
Health Options: Tampa Bay area	16	37	26	84	76	74	82	
Health Options: Jacksonville/Gainesville area	25	41	21	89	83	78	85	
Health Options: Broward/Dade Cos.	14	39	32	86	82	72	79	
Health Options: Orlanda/Central area	12	34	27	75	64	76	84	
Health Options: Escamba/Santa Rosa Cties/Okaloosa	20	47	20	87	82	88	94	
HIP Health Plan of Florida: south Florida and Tampa Bay	19	38	29	85	76	74	81	
Humana Medical Plan: Southeast/Southcentral/Southwest Florida	13	35	29	80	66	69	75	

continued

PLAN NAME	EXTREMELY SATISFIED	VERY SATISFIED	SOMEWHAT SATISFIED	COVERAGE	CHOICE OF DOCTORS	APPOINTMENTS CASE	QUALITY	TOP RATED
Humana Medical Plan: Tampa Bay area	17	33	26	84	65	70	76	
Humana Medical Plan: Jacksonville area	15	32	27	83	62	72	79	
Humana Medical Plan: Daytona area	14	29	27	81	60	78	72	
PCA Family Health Plan of Florida: Most of Florida	12	34	25	82	60	68	79	
PCA Health Plans of Florida: Most of Florida	9	27	31	77	67	70	80	
Prudential HealthCare of Florida: Jacksonville area	31	37	18	90	79	80	90	
Prudential HealthCare HMO: Central Florida area	29	40	18	93	79	84	88	
Prudential HealthCare HMO: Broward/Dade/Palm Beach	22	34	23	85	76	70	80	
Georgia								
Aetna US Healthcare: Atlanta/Augusta/Athens/Macon	16	36	27	87	78	82	87	
Kaiser Permanente: Atlanta area	20	41	28	91	78	89	85	Yes
Prudential HealthCare HMO: Atlanta/Macon areas	13	38	30	84	75	73	81	
Guam								
FHP of Guam	12	33	35	74	66	57	75	
Guam Memorial Health Plan, High:Guam/Palau/N. Marina Isl.	14	30	42	76	75	69	79	
Health Maintenance Life: Guam	15	47	25	76	76	76	83	

continued

CHART 2—HMOS (continued)

PLAN NAME	EXTREMELY SATISFIED	VERY SATISFIED	SOMEWHAT SATISFIED	COVERAGE	CHOICE OF DOCTORS	APPOINTMENTS CASE	QUALITY	TOP RATED
Hawaii								
HMSA's CHP: All of Hawaii	16	40	32	84	87	89	92	
Kaiser Permanente, High:Islands of Hawaii/Maui/Oahu/Kauai	31	37	25	86	83	89	90	Yes
Kaiser Permanente, Std: Islands of Hawaii/Maui/Oahu/Kauai	17	37	32	81	73	90	88	
Idaho								
Group Health NW: Benewah/Bonner/Kootenai/Latah/Shoshone	16	43	27	84	83	84	88	
QualMed WA Health Plan: Northern Idaho/Boise area	15	39	23	79	86	86	95	
Illinois								
Aetna US Healthcare: Chicago area	9	31	32	80	74	76	81	
BCI HMO, Inc.: Chicago/Rockford/Springfield/Downstate Cos.	20	42	20	85	79	80	86	
FHP of Illinois, Inc: Chicago area	17	39	28	83	72	80	86	
Group Health Plan: Southern/Metro East/ Central	15	48	25	88	77	78	86	
Health Alliance HMO: Central/East Central/ NW/West IL	28	39	26	98	82	88	89	Yes
Humana Health Plan: Chicago area	14	33	31	85	64	69	80	
Maxicare Illinois: Chicago/Moline/Peoria/Rockford	12	34	29	82	69	81	89	
Maxicare Illinois: Springfield area	12	37	26	84	65	86	90	

continued

PLAN NAME	EXTREMELY SATISFIED	VERY SATISFIED	SOMEWHAT SATISFIED	COVERAGE	CHOICE OF DOCTORS	APPOINTMENTS CASE	QUALITY	TOP RATED
PARTNERS HMO: St. Louis	25	49	16	90	86	86	89	Yes
PersonalCare's HMO: East Central Illinois	24	45	24	91	80	85	91	Yes
Principal St. Louis: St. Louis area	21	41	26	91	88	85	92	Yes
Rush Prudential HMO: Chicago area	19	41	26	91	77	80	86	
United HealthCare of IL: Chicago area	13	33	30	80	73	72	84	
United HealthCare Select: St. Louis and Metro East	31	40	17	93	86	88	95	
Indiana								
Aetna US Healthcare: Lake/Porter Counties/Indianapolis	9	31	32	80	74	76	81	
BCI HMO, Inc.: Lake and Porter counties	20	42	20	85	79	80	86	
FHP of Illinois: Lake County	17	39	28	83	72	80	86	
Health Alliance HMO: Fountain/Vermillion/Warren Counties	28	39	26	98	82	88	89	Yes
Humana Care Plan: Southern Indiana	20	33	26	84	64	76	81	
Humana Health Plan Inc-Lake City	14	33	31	85	64	69	80	
Humana Health Plan: Southern Indiana	12	39	29	85	74	79	85	
Maxicare Illinois: Lake County	12	34	29	82	69	81	89	
Maxicare Indiana: Most of Indiana	14	40	27	86	77	87	89	
The M*Plan: Central/Northeast/Southwest Indiana	28	46	19	91	86	92	93	Yes

continued

CHART 2—HMOS (continued)

PLAN NAME	EXTREMELY SATISFIED	VERY SATISFIED	SOMEWHAT SATISFIED	COVERAGE	CHOICE OF DOCTORS	APPOINTMENTS CASE	QUALITY	TOP RATED
Prudential HealthCare HMO: Dearborn counties	19	49	21	89	82	86	88	
Rush Prudential HMO: Lake/Porter counties	19	41	26	91	77	80	86	
Wellborn HMO: Evansville area	28	48	17	94	89	95	93	Yes
Iowa								
Care Choices: Northwest Iowa	26	47	23	84	91	90	98	Yes
Exclusive Healthcare: Council Bluffs area	13	41	33	84	86	82	89	
Maxicare Illinois: Clinton/Muscatine/Scott Counties	12	34	29	82	69	81	89	
Principal Health Care of Iowa: Des Moines/Central Iowa/Waterloo	17	36	30	81	79	86	86	
Principal Health Care of NE Iowa: Council Bluffs area	16	38	28	82	80	86	91	
United HealthCare/Midlands: Western Iowa	22	41	24	85	78	81	87	
Kansas								
Kaiser Permanente: Kansas City area	22	43	21	91	74	86	81	
United HealthCare MidWest: Kansas City/Topeka areas	13	46	24	93	94	87	90	
Kentucky								
Advantage Care, Inc.: Central/Eastern Kentucky	35	44	18	93	89	83	95	Yes
Aetna US Healthcare: Northern Kentucky	12	50	24	86	87	88	91	

continued

PLAN NAME	EXTREMELY SATISFIED	VERY SATISFIED	SOMEWHAT SATISFIED	COVERAGE	CHOICE OF DOCTORS	APPOINTMENTS CASE	QUALITY	TOP RATED
Humana Care Plan: Louisville area	20	33	26	84	64	76	81	
Humana Care Plan: Lexington	18	34	30	87	71	86	83	
Humana Health Plan: Lexington/Louisville	12	39	29	85	74	79	85	
PacifiCare of Ohio, Inc: Northern Kentucky	17	41	20	82	79	79	87	
Prudential HealthCare HMO: Northern Kentucky	19	49	21	89	82	86	88	
United HealthCare of Ohio: Most of Ohio	12	44	28	84	83	86	92	
United HealthCare of Kentucky: Most of Kentucky	21	42	25	86	86	85	88	Yes
Louisiana								
Aetna US Healthcare: New Orleans area	19	43	20	85	79	74	86	
United HealthCare of Louisiana: Baton Rouge/Shreveport/Lafayette/Alexander	37	38	16	95	89	89	92	
Maryland								
Aetna US Healthcare: North/Central MD & Washington, DC area	19	36	29	86	76	79	81	
CareFirst: All of Maryland	15	35	34	87	69	77	83	
CIGNA HlthCare Mid-Atlantic: Central/Western MD	15	34	27	86	71	77	81	
George Washington Univ HP, High: Central/Southern MD	23	42	23	92	80	83	89	
George Washington Univ HP, Std: Central/Southern Maryland	12	40	27	88	74	74	83	

continued

CHART 2—HMOS (continued)

PLAN NAME	EXTREMELY SATISFIED	VERY SATISFIED	SOMEWHAT SATISFIED	COVERAGE	CHOICE OF DOCTORS	APPOINTMENTS CASE	QUALITY	TOP RATED
Kaiser Permanente: Baltimore/Washington, DC area	17	35	28	88	77	74	81	
MD-IPA: All of Maryland	19	41	27	88	78	80	90	
NYLCare/Mid-Atlantic-High: North/Central/Southern MD	19	39	26	91	74	82	88	
NYLCare/Mid-Atlantic-Std: North/Central/Southern MD	11	36	32	85	72	75	80	
Massachusetts								
Aetna US Healthcare: Central/Eastern MA/Hampden	20	34	29	89	78	80	91	
CHP/Kaiser Permanente: Western MA	19	44	25	91	84	93	89	
Fallon Community Health Plan: Central/Eastern MA	31	42	19	92	89	94	91	Yes
Harvard Community Hlth Plan: Eastern/Western MA	25	43	20	91	87	88	92	Yes
Harvard Pilgrim Hlth Care, NE: Southeastern MA	22	39	26	88	83	86	86	
Health New England: Western MA	30	48	17	96	86	88	86	
Matthew Thornton Health Plan: Northern MA	26	42	20	90	85	86	91	
Michigan								
Blue Care Network, East MI: Saginaw area	13	43	22	84	67	80	85	
Blue Care Network Health, Center: Mid-Michigan	12	48	30	85	83	90	91	Yes

continued

PLAN NAME	EXTREMELY SATISFIED	VERY SATISFIED	SOMEWHAT SATISFIED	COVERAGE	CHOICE OF DOCTORS	APPOINTMENTS CASE	QUALITY	TOP RATED
Blue Care Network, SE: Detroit/Southeast MI	14	36	29	80	75	80	81	
Blue Care Network, Great Lakes: Southwest Michigan	23	40	23	83	71	80	86	
Blue Care Network, Great Lakes: Western Michigan	20	42	27	87	78	87	89	
CareChoices: Western Michigan	17	53	20	87	84	87	92	
Care Choices: Eastern/Central Michigan area	24	46	21	84	89	88	95	
Health Alliance: Southeastern Michigan/Flint Area	24	39	23	87	79	80	88	
M-Care: Mid/Southeastern MI	35	41	17	91	86	85	92	Yes
OmniCare: Southeastern MI	19	34	30	82	74	65	80	
Physicians Health Plan: Lansing/Mid-Michigan	20	43	25	82	91	93	97	
Physicians Health Plan: Kalamazoo/Southwest Michigan	15	50	26	86	87	83	91	Yes
Priority Health: West Michigan	22	46	24	84	79	87	92	Yes
SelectCare: Southeast Michigan	14	40	26	86	75	80	84	
The Wellness Plan	14	40	26	85	81	79	86	
Minnesota								
HealthPartners Classic, High: Minneapolis/St. Paul areas	19	46	23	87	84	83	90	
HealthPartners Classic, Std: Minneapolis/St. Paul areas	25	45	16	92	83	85	90	

continued

CHART 2—HMOS (continued)

PLAN NAME	EXTREMELY SATISFIED	VERY SATISFIED	SOMEWHAT SATISFIED	COVERAGE	CHOICE OF DOCTORS	APPOINTMENTS CASE	QUALITY	TOP RATED
HealthPartners Health Plan	11	36	30	84	77	81	92	
Medica Primary: Minneapolis/St. Paul areas	11	40	28	85	75	80	86	
Mississippi								
Prudential HealthCare HMO	21	43	23	85	75	79	88	
Missouri								
BlueChoice: St. Louis/Central/Southwest areas	18	42	27	85	78	83	88	
Group Health Plan: St. Louis area	15	48	25	88	77	78	86	
Humana Kansas City, Inc., High: Central Missouri/Springfield area	23	31	26	86	78	81	89	
Humana Kansas City, Inc., High: Kansas City area	23	41	20	91	79	81	89	
Kaiser Permanente: Kansas City area	22	43	21	91	74	86	81	
PARTNERS HMO	25	49	16	90	86	86	89	Yes
Principal St. Louis: St. Louis area	21	41	26	91	88	85	92	Yes
United HealthCare Choice: St. Louis/Centrl/Nrtheast/SE/Joplin	31	52	10	94	93	90	92	Yes
United HealthCare MidWest: Kansas City area	13	46	24	93	94	87	90	
United HealthCare Select: St. Louis/Central/NE/SE	31	40	17	93	86	88	95	

continued

PLAN NAME	EXTREMELY SATISFIED	VERY SATISFIED	SOMEWHAT SATISFIED	COVERAGE	CHOICE OF DOCTORS	APPOINTMENTS CASE	QUALITY	TOP RATED
Nebraska								
Care Choices: Northeastern Nebraska	26	47	23	84	91	90	98	Yes
Exclusive Healthcare: Omaha/Lincoln areas	13	41	33	84	86	82	89	
Principal Health Care of NE: Lincoln/Omaha areas	16	38	28	82	80	86	91	
United HealthCare, Midlands: Lincoln/Omaha/Northeast areas	22	41	24	85	78	81	87	
Nevada								
PacifiCare of Nevada: LasVegas/Laughlin/Reno/Carson Cty/Tahoe	13	27	30	76	56	70	74	
New Hampshire								
CHP/Kaiser Permanente: Southwestern New Hampshire	19	44	25	91	84	93	89	
Harvard Community Hlth Plan: Southern New Hampshire	25	43	20	91	87	88	92	Yes
Matthew Thornton Hlth Plan: All of New Hampshire	26	42	20	90	85	86	91	
New Jersey								
Aetna US Healthcare, High: All of New Jersey	19	35	32	88	89	82	90	
Aetna US Healthcare, Std: All of New Jersey	13	39	32	83	82	84	89	
AmeriHealth HMO: All of New Jersey	12	33	29	82	72	80	83	
First Option Health Plan of NJ: All of New Jersey	24	38	24	85	88	89	92	

continued

CHART 2—HMOS (continued)

PLAN NAME	EXTREMELY SATISFIED	VERY SATISFIED	SOMEWHAT SATISFIED	COVERAGE	CHOICE OF DOCTORS	APPOINTMENTS CASE	QUALITY	TOP RATED
HIP Health Plan of NJ: Most of NJ	16	42	30	95	76	84	88	Yes
NYLCare Health Plans	15	39	27	80	73	76	85	
QualMed Plans for Health: Burlington/Camden/Gloucester Counties	12	33	32	83	73	75	83	
New Mexico								
FHP NM: Albuq/Santa Fe/Farmington/Las Cruces	14	35	27	79	69	71	82	
Lovelace Health Plan: All of New Mexico	24	38	29	87	79	78	90	
QualMed Plans for Health: Albuquerque/Santa Fe areas	22	40	26	88	79	84	87	
New York								
Aetna U.S. Healthcare: NYC area and Dutchess/Sullivan/Ulster Cos	14	37	33	88	76	81	86	
Blue Choice: Rochester area	15	48	27	83	84	89	92	Yes
Blue Choice HMO: Downstate area	17	33	25	85	78	79	88	
Capital District PHP: Capital district area	29	38	18	86	91	89	93	
CHP/Kaiser Permanente: Westchester County	23	41	28	91	86	89	90	
Community Health Plan: Albany/Cooperstown areas	24	41	22	89	82	88	92	
Harvard Community Health Plan: New York adjacent to Massachusetts	23	43	20	91	87	88	92	Yes

continued

PLAN NAME	EXTREMELY SATISFIED	VERY SATISFIED	SOMEWHAT SATISFIED	COVERAGE	CHOICE OF DOCTORS	APPOINTMENTS CASE	QUALITY	TOP RATED
HealthCare Plan: Western New York	17	44	24	88	83	92	90	
HIP of Greater New York: New York City area	15	37	31	86	73	67	82	
HMO-CNY: Syracuse/Binghampton/Elmira areas	23	46	27	91	95	93	97	Yes
Independent Health Associates: Metro Hudson	19	42	25	83	87	88	90	
Independent Health Associates: Western New York	20	45	28	86	88	88	92	Yes
MVP Health Plan: Eastern Region	21	42	25	79	83	94	92	
MVP Health Plan: Central/Northern Region	19	41	29	81	81	89	92	
MVP Health Plan: Mid-Hudson Region	20	48	19	89	88	90	90	
NYLCare Health Plans: New York City area	15	35	27	84	69	70	77	
PHP/Slocum/Dickson: Utica area	24	43	20	88	81	90	93	
Preferred Care: Rochester area	21	51	22	90	88	90	92	Yes
Prepaid Health Plan: Syracuse/Southern Tier areas	24	43	24	87	85	89	93	Yes
Vytra Healthcare: Queens/Nassau/Suffolk Counties	23	50	16	88	88	84	92	
North Carolina								
Kaiser Permanente: Charlotte/Triangle areas	20	40	27	91	83	86	87	
Maxicare North Carolina:Charlotte/Greenboro/Raleigh areas	16	39	28	86	78	85	89	

continued

CHART 2—HMOS (continued)

PLAN NAME	EXTREMELY SATISFIED	VERY SATISFIED	SOMEWHAT SATISFIED	COVERAGE	CHOICE OF DOCTORS	APPOINTMENTS CASE	QUALITY	TOP RATED
Partners NHP of North Carolina: Most of state	25	44	19	87	87	90	91	
Prudential HealthCare HMO: Charlotte/Raleigh areas	23	40	21	82	75	87	87	
UHC of North Carolina: Central/Eastern/Western	16	46	21	82	86	78	91	
North Dakota								
HealthPartners Health Plan: Eastern North Dakota	11	36	30	84	77	81	92	
Ohio								
Advantage Health Plan of Ohio & W. Va.: Eastern Ohio	11	32	28	80	73	87	87	
Aetna US Healthcare: Cleveland/Akron/Cincinnati/Dayton/Columbus	12	50	24	86	87	88	91	
CHP of Ohio: Northeaster/Central/Southern Ohio	23	40	25	91	86	91	89	
CIGNA of Ohio: Columbus area	22	33	29	89	70	79	86	
DayMed Health Maint. Plan: Dayton/Cinn./Columbus/Cleve./Akron	15	34	27	86	87	83	95	
Health Maintenance Plan (HMP): Most of state	23	45	19	86	86	83	91	
Health Plan of Upper Ohio Valley: Eastern Ohio	18	43	23	82	80	85	90	
Health Power HMO: Columbus/Cinncinati/Dayton areas	16	32	25	82	75	84	84	
HMO Health Ohio: Northeast Ohio	16	43	29	84	77	81	84	
HMO Health Ohio: Central Ohio	22	43	19	83	79	78	90	

continued

PLAN NAME	EXTREMELY SATISFIED	VERY SATISFIED	SOMEWHAT SATISFIED	COVERAGE	CHOICE OF DOCTORS	APPOINTMENTS CASE	QUALITY	TOP RATED
Kaiser Permanente: Akron/Cleveland areas	20	36	29	89	73	79	85	
PacifiCare of Ohio: Cincinnati/Dayton	17	41	20	82	79	79	87	
Prudential HealthCare HMO: Central Ohio	21	41	20	86	81	81	89	
Prudential HealthCare HMO: Cleveland/Akron areas	11	35	35	81	78	83	88	
Prudential HealthCare HMO: Cincinnati/Southwest areas	19	49	21	89	82	86	88	
Super Med HMO: Northeast Ohio	19	34	28	82	73	79	87	
United Health Care of Ohio: Cincinnati/Dayton/Springfield/Toledo	12	44	28	84	83	86	92	
United Health Care of Ohio: Central/Northeast/South Central areas	22	45	20	85	87	88	93	
Oklahoma								
BlueLines HMO: Okla. City/Tulsa/Lawton/Southwest Okla. areas	17	37	25	83	79	83	84	
PacifiCare Oklahoma: Okla. City/Southwestern Okla./Tulsa areas	17	27	31	88	66	65	77	
Prudential HealthCare HMO: Central and Western Oklahoma	14	38	30	76	73	80	80	
Prudential HealthCare HMO: Tulsa area	31	40	17	86	81	84	89	
Oregon								
Kaiser Permanente, High: Portland/Salem areas	22	45	24	94	80	89	90	
Kaiser Permanente, Std: Portland/Salem areas	24	44	23	93	76	84	90	
Pacificare of Oregon: Counties along I-5 corridor	12	48	24	80	82	81	89	

continued

CHART 2—HMOS (continued)

PLAN NAME	EXTREMELY SATISFIED	VERY SATISFIED	SOMEWHAT SATISFIED	COVERAGE	CHOICE OF DOCTORS	APPOINTMENTS CASE	QUALITY	TOP RATED
QuadMed Oregon Health Plan: Most of Oregon except Southeast	12	39	22	74	82	81	87	
SelectCare: Western Oregon/I-5 corridor	13	38	26	71	75	79	87	
Pennsylvania								
Advantage Health Plan, Pennsylvania: Pittsburgh area	20	40	23	85	81	74	82	
Aetna U.S. Healthcare, High: Western/Central/Northeastern Penn.	15	40	30	91	80	81	85	
Aetna U.S. Healthcare, High: Philadelphia area	14	45	29	94	89	87	92	
Aetna U.S. Healthcare, Std: Philadelphia area	9	37	33	82	84	82	88	
First Priority Health: Northeastern Pennsylvania	19	36	32	79	86	89	93	
HealthAmerica Pennsylvania: Greater Pittsburgh area	19	45	22	86	80	82	87	
HealthAmerica Pennsylvania: South Central Pennsylvania	24	51	15	89	87	91	92	
HealthGuard: Birks/Cumberland/Dauphine/Lane/Lebanon/York	20	50	19	86	89	94	93	
Keystone Health Plan Central: Harrisburg area	22	39	28	84	86	85	92	
Keystone Health Plan East: Philadelphia area	19	36	27	85	80	78	84	
Keystone Blue: Pittsburgh/Altoona/Erie areas	12	38	28	78	81	78	86	
QualMed Plans for Health: Southern Pennsylvania	12	33	32	83	73	75	83	

continued

PLAN NAME	EXTREMELY SATISFIED	VERY SATISFIED	SOMEWHAT SATISFIED	COVERAGE	CHOICE OF DOCTORS	APPOINTMENTS CASE	QUALITY	TOP RATED
Rhode Island								
Harvard Community Health Plan: Northeast Rhode Island	25	43	20	91	87	88	92	Yes
Harvard-Pilgrim Health Care Northeast: Whole state	22	39	26	88	83	86	88	
South Carolina								
Companion HealthCare: Coastal/Midlands/PeeDee/Piedmont areas	13	33	34	81	79	86	92	
Kaiser Permanente: Rock Hill area	20	40	27	91	83	86	87	
MaxiCare North Carolina: Chester/York Counties	16	39	28	86	78	85	89	
MaxiCare North Carolina: Columbia/Greenville/Spartenburg areas	6	42	31	79	70	85	88	
Partners NHP of North Carolina: Upstate South Carolina	25	44	19	87	87	90	91	
Prudential HealthCare HMO: York County	23	40	21	82	75	87	87	
South Dakota								
Care Choices: Clay/Union Counties	26	47	23	84	91	90	98	Yes
Tennessee								
Healthsource Tennessee: Knox/Nash/Chatanooga/Memphis/Tri City	13	38	29	81	84	82	90	
Prudential HealthCare HMO: Nashville area	17	40	26	83	76	74	87	
Prudential HealthCare HMO: Memphis area	21	43	23	85	75	79	88	
United HealthCare of Tennessee: Chatanooga/Memphis/Nashville	21	39	28	89	85	80	86	

continued

CHART 2—HMOS (continued)

PLAN NAME	EXTREMELY SATISFIED	VERY SATISFIED	SOMEWHAT SATISFIED	COVERAGE	CHOICE OF DOCTORS	APPOINTMENTS CASE	QUALITY	TOP RATED
Texas								
Aetna U.S. Healthcare: Dallas/Ft. Worth areas	17	42	29	87	80	80	84	
FHP New Mexico: El Paso area	14	35	27	79	69	71	82	
FirstCare: West Texas	29	35	24	91	77	81	89	
Harris Methodist: Dallas/Ft. Worth area	19	46	22	90	81	77	89	
Humana Health Plan of Texas: Houston area	15	34	29	84	70	79	81	
Humana Health Plan of Texas: San Antonio area	16	33	26	81	65	69	79	
Humana of Corpus Christi: Corpus Christi area	20	36	25	81	61	73	84	
Kaiser Permanente: Dallas/Ft. Worth area	22	31	23	85	65	80	76	
NYLCare Health Plans SW: Dallas/Ft. Worth/East and West Texas	18	42	21	86	72	75	83	
NYLCare Health Plan of the Gulf Coast: Houston area	19	37	25	86	75	76	84	
NYLCare H. P. of Gulf Coast: Austin/C.Christi/S.Antonio/Vict.	3	39	28	79	74	71	88	
PacifiCare of Texas: S. Antonio/Hstn./Galv./Dallas/Ft. Wth/G. Coast	20	35	26	85	72	57	76	
PCA Health Plans of Texas: Austin/Dallas/Houston/S. Ant./C.Christi	22	37	24	87	77	78	85	
Principal HealthCare of Texas: Corpus Christi area	17	44	20	79	83	80	86	
Prudential HealthCare HMO: Austin area	18	39	22	86	66	75	80	

continued

PLAN NAME	EXTREMELY SATISFIED	VERY SATISFIED	SOMEWHAT SATISFIED	COVERAGE	CHOICE OF DOCTORS	APPOINTMENTS CASE	QUALITY	TOP RATED
Prudential HealthCare HMO: Houston area	20	37	25	89	73	68	81	
Prudential HealthCare HMO: San Antonio area	32	37	21	87	81	84	86	Yes
Scott and White: Austin/Bryan/Coll.Station/Killeen/Temple/Waco	27	48	16	96	89	77	95	
United HealthCare of Texas: Dallas/Ft. Worth area	14	40	32	86	83	85	90	
Utah								
IHC: Northeastern/Northwestern Utah	12	41	24	83	87	83	91	
PacifiCare of Utah: Wasatch front/Washington County	13	41	32	87	78	74	87	
Vermont								
Harvard Community Health Plan: Southern Vermont	25	43	20	91	87	88	92	
MVP Health Plan: Bennington/Chittenden/Rutland/Wash. Cos.	14	45	25	83	81	91	95	
Virginia								
Aetna US Healthcare: Northern Virginia area	19	36	29	86	76	79	81	
Aetna US Healthcare: Richmond/Tri-City areas	17	41	23	87	73	85	86	
CIGNA HealthCare Virginia: Southeastern Virginia	23	41	22	87	86	81	87	
CIGNA HealthCare of Virginia: Central Virginia	23	45	23	83	80	83	89	
CIGNA HealthCare Mid-Atlantic: Northern Virginia	15	34	27	86	71	77	81	
G.W. Univ. H.P., High: Fredericksburg/DC areas	23	42	23	92	80	83	89	

continued

CHART 2 — HMOS (continued)

PLAN NAME	EXTREMELY SATISFIED	VERY SATISFIED	SOMEWHAT SATISFIED	COVERAGE	CHOICE OF DOCTORS	APPOINTMENTS CASE	QUALITY	TOP RATED
G. W. Univ. H.P., Std: Fredericksburg/DC areas	12	40	27	88	74	74	83	
Healthkeepers: Richmd/Cville/Frburg/Hamp. Roads/Roanoke areas	17	45	29	79	83	85	91	
Kaiser Permanente: Washington, D.C. area	17	35	28	88	77	74	81	
MD-IPA: N. Va./Central Va./Richmond/Tidewater/Roanoke	19	41	27	88	78	80	90	
NYLCare/Mid-Atlantic, High: N. Va./F'burg/Richmond/Tri-Cities	19	39	26	91	74	82	88	
NYLCare/Mid-Atlantic, Std: N. Va./F'burg/Richmond/Tri-Cities	11	36	32	85	72	75	80	
Optima Health Plan: Peninsula/Southside Hampton Roads	20	43	23	86	84	83	92	
Partners NHP of North Carolina: Southeast Virginia	25	44	19	87	87	90	91	
Priority Health Care: Southside Hampton Roads	14	42	28	90	90	88	93	
Prudential HealthCare HMO: Richmond/Tri-City areas	16	35	32	86	74	83	86	
Washington								
Group Health Coop. of Puget Sound, High: Most of Western Washington	23	41	20	88	77	83	85	
Group Health Coop. of P. Sound, Std: Most of West. Washington	16	43	26	88	79	84	85	
Group Health Northwest: Central Wash./Spokane/Colville/Pullman	16	43	27	84	83	84	88	
Kaiser Permanente, High: Vancouver/Longview	22	45	24	94	80	89	90	Yes

continued

PLAN NAME	EXTREMELY SATISFIED	VERY SATISFIED	SOMEWHAT SATISFIED	COVERAGE	CHOICE OF DOCTORS	APPOINTMENTS CASE	QUALITY	TOP RATED
Kaiser Permanente, Std: Vancouver/Longview	24	44	23	93	76	84	89	Yes
Kitsap Physicians Service, High: Kitsap/Mason/Jefferson Counties	25	43	17	90	91	88	92	
Kitsap Physicians Service, Std: Kitsap/Mason/Jefferson Counties	26	50	19	90	94	91	97	Yes
PacifiCare of Oregon: Clark County	12	48	24	80	82	81	91	
PacifiCare of Wash.: Puget Sound/Most West. Wash./Parts E. Wash.	17	37	32	82	78	79	87	
QualMed Oregon Health Plan: Clark/Cowlitz Counties	12	39	22	74	82	81	87	
QualMed Washington H.P.: Most of state	15	39	23	79	86	86	95	
SelectCare: Lower Columbian Basin	13	38	26	71	75	79	87	
West Virginia								
Advantage Health Plan, Ohio & W. Va.: Panhandle/N. Cent./Charl. area	11	32	28	80	73	87	87	
Health Plan of Upper Ohio Valley: No./Central W. Va.	18	43	23	82	80	85	90	
Wisconsin								
Compcare Health Services: Southeastern Wisconsin	11	37	32	84	80	85	88	
Family Health Plan: Milwaukee area	19	42	25	93	76	85	87	
Group Health Coop.: Greater Dane and Jefferson Counties	30	39	27	95	80	88	92	Yes
HealthPartners Classic, High: Pierce/St. Croix Counties	19	46	23	87	84	83	90	

continued

CHART 2—HMOS (continued)

PLAN NAME	EXTREMELY SATISFIED	VERY SATISFIED	SOMEWHAT SATISFIED	COVERAGE	CHOICE OF DOCTORS	APPOINTMENTS CASE	QUALITY	TOP RATED
HealthPartners Classic, Std: Pierce/St. Croix Counties	25	45	16	92	83	85	90	
HealthPartners Health Plan: West Central Wisconsin	11	36	30	84	77	81	92	
Humana Wisconsin Health Org.: Southeastern Wisconsin	12	35	31	80	82	88	92	
PrimeCare Health Plan: Southeastern Wisconsin	14	42	23	82	80	84	92	
Unity Health Plans: Southern/Central Wisconsin	12	41	26	80	72	81	93	

POINT-OF-SERVICE PLANS

PLAN NAME	EXTREMELY SATISFIED	VERY SATISFIED	SOMEWHAT SATISFIED	COVERAGE	CHOICE OF DOCTORS	APPOINTMENTS CASE	QUALITY	TOP RATED
Arizona								
Health Plan of Nevada: Mojave County	12	31	33	80	71	62	78	
Arkansas								
American HMO: Most of Arkansas	21	33	26	82	80	83	89	
Colorado								
HMO Colorado/Nevada: Most of CO	19	36	34	85	80	88	92	
Connecticut								
Physicians Health Services CT	25	40	22	86	90	90	92	
Delaware								
Prudential HealthCare HMO	18	45	20	88	80	85	92	
United HealthCare Mid-Atlantic: DC/most MD	16	38	28	87	77	78	86	
Georgia								
United Health Care/GA: Atlanta, NW GA	16	42	27	90	84	84	88	
Hawaii								
HMSA: All of Hawaii	22	45	23	86	93	89	95	Yes

continued

POINT-OF-SERVICE PLANS (continued)

PLAN NAME	EXTREMELY SATISFIED	VERY SATISFIED	SOMEWHAT SATISFIED	COVERAGE	CHOICE OF DOCTORS	APPOINTMENTS CASE	QUALITY	TOP RATED
Idaho								
HMO Blue: SW/Nrthern/E. Idaho	11	46	26	77	80	86	86	
Illinois								
American HMO: Chicago area/Central/So/Wstern IL	19	32	29	86	72	78	89	
Indiana								
American HMO: Northwest IN	19	32	29	86	72	78	89	
Louisiana								
Maxicare LA: Baton Rouge/New Orleans area	20	37	28	85	82	68	84	
Maryland								
Columbia Medical Plan:Central MD	23	41	23	95	82	78	88	
Free State Health Plan:All of MD	25	39	24	92	82	78	91	
Prudential HealthCare HMO: Most of MD	18	45	20	88	80	85	92	
United HealthCare Mid-Atlantic: Most MD/DC	16	38	28	87	77	78	86	
Massachusetts								
Coordinated Health Partners:SE MA	26	41	22	90	87	90	93	
United HealthCare New England: All of MA	25	40	27	86	91	86	93	Yes

continued

PLAN NAME	EXTREMELY SATISFIED	VERY SATISFIED	SOMEWHAT SATISFIED	COVERAGE	CHOICE OF DOCTORS	APPOINTMENTS CASE	QUALITY	TOP RATED
Nevada								
Health Plan of Nevada: Las Vegas/Reno areas	12	31	33	80	71	62	78	
New Jersey								
GHI Health Plan: No. NJ	11	31	35	73	75	80	85	
New Mexico								
Presbyterian Health Plan: Most of NM	23	41	21	88	80	76	87	
New York								
Community Blue: Western NY	13	46	27	87	91	90	93	
GHI Health Plan	11	31	35	73	75	80	85	
Oxford Health Plans	18	35	27	84	87	84	89	
Pennsylvania								
Free State Health Plan: So. PA	25	39	24	92	82	78	91	
Penn State Geisinger HlthPlans	25	41	25	88	81	84	90	Yes
Puerto Rico								
Triple-S	26	47	19	90	92	79	91	Yes
Rhode Island								
Coordinated Health Partners	26	41	22	90	87	90	93	
United HealthCare New England	25	40	27	86	91	86	93	Yes

continued

POINT-OF-SERVICE PLANS (continued)

PLAN NAME	EXTREMELY SATISFIED	VERY SATISFIED	SOMEWHAT SATISFIED	COVERAGE	CHOICE OF DOCTORS	APPOINTMENTS CASE	QUALITY	TOP RATED
Virginia								
Prudential HealthCare HMO	18	45	20	88	80	85	92	
United HealthCare Mid-Atlantic	16	38	28	87	77	78	86	
West Virginia								
Free State Health Plan	25	39	24	92	82	78	91	

APPENDIX C

Millions of Medicare recipients are joining Medicare HMOs and considering other new alternatives to the traditional Medicare program. With this vast migration out of the conventional program taking place, the Families USA Foundation, a Washington-based health care consumer organization, studied one measure that may help indicate levels of member satisfaction with different plans. The group studied data from 1995 through the first four months of 1997 and analyzed the voluntary disenrollment rates for Medicare HMOs. This is the rate by which members left plans during a given year. Families USA also came up with figures for the "rapid disenrollment rate," or the percentage of a plan's disenrollees who cancelled their applications before coverage became effective or cancelled the coverage itself within three months.

The figures are not conclusive and you should use them in conjunction with other material you are assembling. A high voluntary disenrollment rate may indicate widespread dissatisfaction with a plan, but it can also be a result of marketing problems or poor market conditions. A high rapid disenrollment rate could mean that Medicare recipients did not understand the ramifications of leaving the traditional program or that marketing agents provided them false or inaccurate information. Families USA believes that a high rapid disenrollment rate should not be viewed as a problem in a plan with a low overall disenrollment rate. Families USA also monitors member complaints with health care coverage and the progress of state and Federal health care legislation, You can reach the organization at 202-628-3030 or on the Internet at www.familiesusa.org, or by writing to the organization at 1334 G Street NW, 3d floor, Washington, D.C. 20005.

COMPARING MEDICARE HMO'S

MEDICARE DISENROLLMENT DATA BY PLAN — 1996*

CONTRACT	PLAN NAME	DISENROLLMENT RATE	RAPID DISENROLLMENT RATE
Alabama	HealthPartners Alabama	10.7%	33.3%
	United HealthCare of AL (Jefferson, Shelby)	16.2%	57.7%
	United HealthCare of AL (Mobile)	21.3%	52.2%
Arizona	FHP	9.2%	11.6%
	Humana (Phoenix)	21.3%	21.7%
	Maricopa County Health Plan	16.4%	33.0%
	Intergroup	11.8%	25.9%
	HealthPartners	7.3%	22.0%
	Cigna HealthCare of Arizona (Phoenix)	9.7%	21.6%
California	AETNA HP of California (S. CA)	13.8%	13.4%
	Kaiser Los Angeles	3.8%	29.8%
	Kaiser Bakersfield	6.1%	35.1%
	PacifiCare (S. CA)	8.8%	13.7%
	Intervalley Health (S. CA)	11.9%	5.3%
	Aetna HP of California (N. CA)	7.1%	19.4%
	CareAmerica (S. CA)	20.1%	28.1%
	Foundation Health (S. CA)	32.6%	17.3%
	Maxicare (S. CA)	26.6%	37.0%
	PacifiCare (N. CA)	11.3%	26.6%
	Health Net (N. CA)	12.7%	12.1%
	Health Net (S. CA)	15.6%	17.0%
	Blue Cross California (S. CA)	39.9%	61.1%
	HealthPlan of Redwoods (N. CA)	8.7%	20.2%
	National Med Enterprises (N. CA)	6.9%	20.8%
	Health Net Central Valley	52.1%	4.2%
	Prudential (S. CA)	28.2%	36.9%
	Prudential (N. CA)	20.4%	34.1%

*Source: HCFA, *Monthly Disenrollment Patterns Report*, 1996: HCFA, TEFRA Risk Contracts as of Period: 3/97.

**These plans split in two some time during the year. We estimated membership and disenrollment numbers based on previous months' data and information from the new plans period. Thus, the numbers for these plans are estimates only. We have erred on the side of favoring the plans. See Methodology.

COMPARING MEDICARE HMO'S (continued)

MEDICARE DISENROLLMENT DATA BY PLAN—1996*

CONTRACT	PLAN NAME	DISENROLLMENT RATE	RAPID DISENROLLMENT RATE
	FHP (N. CA)	19.5%	41.7%
	Cigna Glendale (S. CA)	19.9%	38.3%
	Kaiser Oakland (N. CA)	2.6%	30.0%
	Kaiser Oakland (Central CA)	5.6%	45.7%
	Foundation Health (N. CA)	14.2%	23.4%
	Lifeguard (N. CA)	19.7%	58.3%
	PacifiCare (N. CA)	12.7%	46.9%
	Watts Health Foundation (S. CA)	26.0%	24.4%
	FHP (S. CA)	14.5%	11.8%
	SCAN Health Plan (S. CA)	27.4%	40.6%
Colorado	HMO Colorado	23.4%	31.9%
	FHP Colorado	10.4%	34.8%
	QualMed Denver	16.7%	19.1%
	Kaiser Foundation HP of Colorado	6.1%	24.0%
	Cigna HealthCare of Colorado	32.1%	32.5%
Connecticut	US Healthcare, Conn.	16.0%	55.7%
Delaware	US Healthcare, Delaware	17.3%	47.4%
District of Columbia	Humana	31.6%	51.7%
Florida	Foundation Health	38.7%	28.3%
	AvMed Health Miami	14.8%	35.7%
	Health Options, S. FL	15.0%	25.2%
	Florida Health	7.1%	15.5%
	Humana	21.3%	23.1%
	PCA, Miami	46.7%	35.2%
	AvMed Health, Gainesville	24.5%	10.7%
	AvMed Health, Jacksonville	48.2%	16.0%
	AvMed Health, Orlando	62.0%	13.1%

COMPARING MEDICARE HMO'S (continued)

MEDICARE DISENROLLMENT DATA BY PLAN—1996*

CONTRACT	PLAN NAME	DISENROLLMENT RATE	RAPID DISENROLLMENT RATE
	AvMed Health, Tampa	46.7%	14.4%
	PCA, Tampa	60.1%	22.9%
	PCA, Jacksonville	81.1%	17.1%
	Prudential, Jacksonville	15.7%	48.7%
	Health Options (Northeast FL)	38.1%	25.3%
	Prudential (S. FL)	20.8%	39.0%
	Prudential, Tampa	13.9%	48.0%
	HIP (S. Florida)	38.2%	53.9%
	Neighborhood Health (S. FL)	26.4%	65.3%
	Prudential, Orlando	11.2%	45.3%
	HIP (West Central FL)	17.8%	53.2%
	Cigna Tampa	27.4%	58.4%
	United HealthCare (S. FL)	18.8%	28.6%
Hawaii	Kaiser Honolulu	2.7%	10.4%
Illinois	Humana Health Plan	17.7%	34.2%
	Health District	36.7%	59.7%
	United HealthCare of Illinois	11.3%	28.8%
Indiana	Maxicare Indiana	9.1%	19.2%
Kentucky	Humana Health Plan	21.8%	43.8%
Louisianna	Ochsner Health	12.4%	27.8%
	Community Health Network	29.9%	44.8%
	Gulf South	12.7%	61.3%
Maryland	Healthcare Corp. of Mid-Atlantic	21.3%	86.5%
	United HealthCare, Mid-Atlantic	13.4%	66.1%
	NYLCare	12.3%	48.5%
	US Healthcare MD	15.6%	50.6%

COMPARING MEDICARE HMO'S (continued)

MEDICARE DISENROLLMENT DATA BY PLAN—1996*

CONTRACT	PLAN NAME	DISENROLLMENT RATE	RAPID DISENROLLMENT RATE
Massachusetts	Harvard Community Health Plan	4.7%	34.8%
	Tufts	7.2%	47.1%
	Pilgrim Health Plan	9.8%	46.7%
	Fallon Community Health	2.4%	10.4%
	US Healthcare MA	16.1%	45.5%
Michigan	Health Alliance*	10.8%	64.9%
	Blue Care Network	2.8%	28.8%
Minnesota	Group Health (now HealthPartners)	4.1%	12.1%
	Medico	4.2%	9.1%
Missouri	Humana Kansas City	13.8%	36.2%
	Total Health Care	30.8%	1.0%
	United HealthCare of the Midwest	11.7%	49.6%
	Good Health HMO	29.4%	61.0%
	HMO Missouri (Alliance BCBS)	15.7%	34.1%
	Group Health Plan	5.2%	66.0%
Nebraska	United HealthCare	10.2%	22.3%
Nevada	Health Plan of Nevada	16.8%	30.5%
	FHP Nevada	17.2%	10.8%
	Humana Health Plan	32.5%	56.5%
	Hometown Health Plan	11.7%	46.1%
New Jersey	Oxford Health NJ	12.9%	61.0%
	HMO, NJ	14.3%	47.0%
	AmeriHealth	18.4%	77.8%
	HIP	9.5%	49.9%
New Mexico	FHP NEW Mexico	7.2%	14.0%
	QualMed New Medico	15.4%	22.2%

COMPARING MEDICARE HMO'S (continued)

MEDICARE DISENROLLMENT DATA BY PLAN — 1996*

CONTRACT	PLAN NAME	DISENROLLMENT RATE	RAPID DISENROLLMENT RATE
	Presbyterian Health	6.9%	17.8%
	Lovelace Health Plan	5.8%	23.9%
New York	Rochester Area HMO	4.0%	19.6%
	Oxford Health	10.2%	43.7%
	US Healthcare NY	17.1%	44.3%
	HIP of Greater NY	7.4%	23.0%
	Health Care Plan	6.3%	46.4%
	NYLCare	20.5%	7.5%
	Managed Health	12.7%	8.9%
	Vytra Healthcare	12.4%	60.6%
	Wellcare of New York	17.7%	52.2%
	Kaiser	8.4%	65.9%
Ohio	Kaiser Foundation Health Plan	6.2%	32.5%
	Family Health Plan	7.8%	10.7%
	Paramount Care	5.0%	3.3%
	Prudential of N. Ohio	18.6%	43.7%
	Community Insurance	18.2%	71.1%
	Aetna Health Plan of Ohio	14.5%	41.8%
Oklahoma	Pacificare Oklahoma	10.4%	41.1%
Oregon	PacifiCare Oregon	10.1%	16.2%
	Providence Health S. Oregon	6.6%	28.4%
	HMO Oregon	8.6%	24.9%
	Selectcare Lower Columbia	10.6%	22.2%
	Selectcare West Central	7.4%	47.8%
	Kaiser Northwest	7.2%	8.5%
	Providence Health OR (Northwest)	5.4%	30.6%
Pennsylvania	US Healthcare Systems	7.0%	41.0%
	QualMed	14.7%	27.0%

COMPARING MEDICARE HMO'S (continued)

MEDICARE DISENROLLMENT DATA BY PLAN—1996*

CONTRACT	PLAN NAME	DISENROLLMENT RATE	RAPID DISENROLLMENT RATE
	US Healthcare, Pitts.	10.2%	38.0%
	Keystone East	7.1%	47.0%
	HMO of NE PA	9.5%	48.9%
	Geisinger	6.4%	73.8%
	Aetna Central PA	20.0%	32.2%
	Keystone West	8.0%	64.7%
Rhode Island	United HealthCare	5.8%	26.4%
	Harvard Community Health	8.3%	53.9%
Texas	Humana (Corpus Christi)	15.6%	29.9%
	NYLCare (Dallas)	13.0%	33.1%
	Humana (San Antonio)	27.1%	39.6%
	PCA (Austin)	43.9%	43.5%
	NYLCare (Houston)	10.6%	25.6%
	Harris Health Plan (Fort Worth)	10.7%	39.3%
	Prudential (San Antonio)	49.0%	56.1%
	FHP Texas (Houston)	45.7%	50.3%
	Prudential (Houston)	38.7%	42.6%
	PacifiCare Texas (San Antonio)	15.0%	22.2%
Virginia	Sentora	16.1%	19.9%
Washington	PacifiCare	8.9%	30.2%
	Group Health Puget Sound	5.1%	19.0%
	Providence Health WA	10.7%	31.1%
	QualMed Inland Northwest	10.4%	21.6%
Wisconson	Primecare Health	11.4%	65.3%

APPENDIX D

The General Motors Corporation is a national leader in studying and rating managed care plans. It has analyzed the quality and cost of more than 130 plans open to its 230,000 employees in various parts of the country and rewards workers who choose top quality plans by picking up a higher proportion of their premiums. If an employee chooses a poorly rated plan, he or she can wind up paying roughly ten times as much in premium charges because of GM's monetary incentive program. The company selected fifteen plans in 1998 as its "Benchmark Plans"—those whose practices set a standard for others. These are the fifteen:

These Kaiser Permanente plans: Southern California, Northern California, Colorado, Connecticut, Mid-Atlantic, Kansas City, New York, Ohio, Northwest, and Texas.

APPENDIX D

Group Health Northwest

Group Health Cooperative of Puget Sound

Fallon Community Health Plan

Harvard Pilgrim Health Care

CIGNA Lovelace Health Plan

APPENDIX E

HMO REGULATORS

ALABAMA

Alabama Insurance Department
Consumer Services Division
135 Union Street
P.O. Box 303351
Montgomery, AL 36130-3351
(334) 269-3550

Alabama Department of Public Health
Division of Managed Care Compliance
P.O. Box 303017
Montgomery, AL 36130-3017
Phone: (334) 206-5366
Fax: (334) 206-5303

ALASKA

Alaska Division of Insurance
800 East Diamond, Suite 560
Anchorage, AK 99515
(907) 269-7900

ARIZONA

Arizona Department of Insurance
2910 North 44th Street, Suite 210
Phoenix, AZ 85018-7256
Phone: (602) 912-8444
Fax: (602) 912-8469

APPENDIX E

ARKANSAS

Arkansas Insurance Department
Seniors Insurance Network
1123 South University Avenue, Suite 400
Little Rock, AR 72204
(800) 852-5494

Arkansas Department of Health
4815 West Markham Street
Little Rock, AR 72205
Phone: (501) 661-2201
Fax: (501) 671-1450

CALIFORNIA

California Department of Corporations
Health Plan Division
980 9th Street, Suite 500
Sacramento, CA 95814
(800) 400-0815

COLORADO

Colorado Insurance Division
1560 Broadway, Suite 850
Denver, CO 80202
(303) 894-7499, extension 356

Colorado Department of Public Health and Environment
4300 Cherry Creek Drive, South
Denver, CO 80222
(303) 692-2100

CONNECTICUT

Connecticut Insurance Department
P.O. Box 816
Hartford, CT 06142-0816
(860) 297-3863

DELAWARE

Delaware Insurance Department
Rodney Building
841 Silver Lake Boulevard
Dover, DE 19904
(800) 282-8611 or
(302) 739-4251

DISTRICT OF COLUMBIA

District of Columbia Insurance Administration
Department of Consumer and Regulatory Affairs

APPENDIX E

613 G Street, NW, Room 600
Washington, DC 20001
(202) 727-8000

FLORIDA

Florida Department of
Insurance
200 East Gaines Street
Tallahassee, FL 32399-0300
(850) 922-3100

Florida Agency for Health
Care Administration
2727 Mahan Drive
Tallahassee, FL 32308
Phone: (888) 419-3456
Fax: (850) 414-5418

GEORGIA

Georgia Insurance
Department
2 Martin Luther King, Jr.
Drive
716 West Tower
Atlanta, GA 30334
(404) 656-2056

Department of Human
Resources
Division of Public Health
2 Peachtree Street NW

Atlanta, GA 30303-3186
(404) 657-2700

HAWAII

State of Hawaii Insurance
Division
Dept. of Commerce and
Consumer Affairs
P.O. 3614
Honolulu, HI 96811
Phone: (808) 586-2790
Fax: (808) 586-2806

IDAHO

Idaho Insurance
Department
SHIBA Program
700 West State Street, Third
Floor
Boise, ID 83720-0043
(208) 334-4350

ILLINOIS

Illinois Insurance
Department
320 West Washington Street,
Fourth Floor
Springfield, IL 62767
(217) 782-4515

APPENDIX E

INDIANA
Indiana Insurance Department
311 West Washington Street, Suite 300
Indianapolis, IN 46204
(800) 622-4461 or
(317) 232-2385

IOWA
Iowa Insurance Division
Lucas State Office Building
East 12th and Grand Streets, Sixth Floor
Des Moines, IA 50319
(515) 281-5705

KANSAS
Kansas Insurance Department
420 SW Ninth Street
Topeka, KS 66612
(800) 432-2484 or
(913) 296-3071

KENTUCKY
Kentucky Insurance Department
215 West Main Street
Frankfort, KY 40602
(800) 595-6053 or
(502) 564-3630

LOUISIANA
Louisiana Department of Insurance
P.O. Box 94214
Baton Rouge, LA 70804-9214
(800) 259-5301 or
(504) 342-5301

Louisiana Department of Health and Hospitals
1201 Capitol Access Road, P.O. Box 629
Baton Rouge, LA 70821-0629
(504) 342-1532
(504) 342-3738

MAINE
Maine Bureau of Insurance
34 State House Station
Augusta, ME 04333-0034
(207) 624-8475
(207) 624-8599

MARYLAND
Maryland Insurance Administration
Compliance and Investigation

APPENDIX E

Unit—Life and Health
501 St. Paul Place
Baltimore, MD 21202-2272
(410) 468-2000
(410) 764-8489

Maryland Department of
Health and Mental Hygiene
201 Preston Street,
Fifth Floor
Baltimore, MD 21201
(410) 767-6860
(410) 764-8489

MASSACHUSETTS

Massachusetts Insurance
Division
Consumer Services Section
470 Atlantic Avenue
Boston, MA 02210-2223
(617) 521-7777

MICHIGAN

Department of Commerce
Law Building, Fourth Floor
P.O. Box 30004
Lansing, MI 48909
(517) 373-7230

Michigan Department of
Community Health

Lewis Cass Building,
Sixth Floor
320 South Walnut Street
Lansing, MI 48913
(517) 335-3500

MINNESOTA

Minnesota Department of
Health
Managed Care Section
Metro Square Building,
Suite 400
121 East Seventh Place
St. Paul, MN 55101
(612) 282-5000
(612) 282-5628

MISSISSIPPI

Mississippi State Department
of Health
2423 North State Street
P.O. Box 1700
Jackson, MS 39215-1700
(601) 960-7680
(601) 354-6794

MISSOURI

Missouri Department of
Insurance

| 255 |

P.O. Box 690
Jefferson City, MO 65102-0690
(573) 751-4126

MONTANA

Montana Insurance Department
126 North Sanders
Mitchell Bldg., Room 270
P.O. Box 4009
Helena, MT 59601
(406) 444-2040

NEBRASKA

Nebraska Department of Insurance
941 O Street, Suite 400
Lincoln, NE 68508
(402) 471-2201
(402) 471-4610

NEVADA

Nevada Department of Business and Industry
Division of Insurance
Consumer Services
1665 Hot Springs Road, No. 152
Carson City, NV 89706
(702) 687-7650
(702) 687-3937

NEW HAMPSHIRE

New Hampshire Insurance Department
Life and Health Division
169 Manchester Street
Concord, NH 03301
(800) 852-3416 or
(603) 271-2261

NEW JERSEY

New Jersey Insurance Department
20 West State Street
Roebling Bldg.
C N 325
Trenton, NJ 08625
(609) 292-5363

New Jersey Department of Health
Office of Managed Care
P.O. Box 360
Trenton, NJ 08625
(609) 633-0660
(609) 633-0807

APPENDIX E

NEW MEXICO

New Mexico Insurance
Department
P.O. Drawer 1269
Santa Fe, NM 87504-1269
(505) 827-4601

NEW YORK

New York Insurance
Department
160 West Broadway
New York, NY 10013
(212) 480-6400 or
(statewide) (800) 342-3736

OREGON

Insurance Division of the
State of Oregon
Consumer Protection Division
350 Winter Street NE
Salem, OR 97310
(503) 947-7984
(503) 378-4351

PENNSYLVANIA

Pennsylvania Insurance
Department
Consumer Services Bureau
1321 Strawberry Square

Harrisburg, PA 17120
(717) 787-2317
Department of Health
Bureau of Managed Care
P.O. Box 90, Room 1030
Harrisburg, PA 17108
(717) 787-5193
(717) 705-0947

PUERTO RICO

Puerto Rico Office of the
Commissioner of Insurance
P.O. Box 8330
San Juan, PR 00910-8330
(787) 722-8686

RHODE ISLAND

Rhode Island Department of
Health
Health Services Regulation
3 Capitol Hill
Providence, RI 02908
(401) 222-6015
(401) 222-3017

SOUTH CAROLINA

South Carolina Department
of Insurance
Consumer Affairs Section

APPENDIX E

P.O. Box 100105
Columbia, SC 29202-3105
(803) 737-6160

SOUTH DAKOTA

South Dakota Insurance Department
500 East Capitol Avenue
Pierre, SD 57501-5070
(605) 773-3563

South Dakota Department of Health
Licensure and Certification
615 East Fourth Street
Pierre, SD 57501
(605) 773-3356
(605) 773-6667

TENNESSEE

Tennessee Department of Commerce and Insurance
Insurance Assistance Office
500 James Robertson Parkway
Nashville, TN 37243
(615) 741-2218
(615) 532-7389

TEXAS

Texas Department of Insurance

H.M.O. Division
333 Guadalupe
Austin, TX 78701
(512) 322-4266
(512) 322-4260

UTAH

Utah Insurance Department
Consumer Services
3110 State Office Building
Salt Lake City, UT 84114-6901
(801) 538-3805
(801) 538-3829

VERMONT

Vermont Division of Health Care Administration
89 Main Street, Drawer 20
Montpelier, VT 05620-3101
(802) 828-2900
(802) 828-2949

VIRGINIA

Virginia Bureau of Insurance
1300 East Main Street, Room 214
Richmond, VA 23219
(804) 371-9694

Virginia Department of Health

APPENDIX E

Center For Quality Health Care Services and Consumer Protection
Division of Acute Care Services
3600 West Broad Street, Suite 216
Richmond, VA 23230
(804) 367-2102
(804) 367-2149

WASHINGTON

Washington State Office of the Insurance Commissioner
P.O. Box 40255
Olympia, WA 98504-0255
(800) 397-4422 or
(360) 753-3613
(360) 586-3535

WEST VIRGINIA

West Virginia Insurance Department
Consumer Services
P.O. Box 50540
Charleston, WV 25305-0540
(800) 642-9004 or (hearing impaired) (800) 435-7381 or
(304) 558-3386

WISCONSIN

State of Wisconsin Office of the Commissioner of Insurance
121 East Wilson Street
Madison, WI 53702
(608) 266-3585
(608) 266-9935

WYOMING

Wyoming Insurance Department
Herschler Building
3d Floor East
122 West Twenty-fifth Street
Cheyenne, WY 82002-0440
(307) 777-6887
(307) 777-5895

APPENDIX F

State insurance hot lines provide help on a wide range of insurance matters, including Medicare.

STATE INSURANCE COUNSELING

STATE	PHONE NUMBER
ALABAMA	(800) 243-5463
ALASKA	(907) 562-7249
ARIZONA	(800) 432-4040
	(602) 542-6595
ARKANSAS	(800) 852-5494
	(501) 686-2640
CALIFORNIA	(800) 434-0222 (HICAP Hot line)
	(916) 323-7315
COLORADO	(800) 544-9181
	(303) 894-7499, Ext. 356
DELAWARE	(800) 336-9500
	(302) 739-6266
DISTRICT OF COLUMBIA	(202) 676-3900

STATE INSURANCE COUNSELING (cont.)

STATE	PHONE NUMBER
FLORIDA	(800) 963-5337
GEORGIA	(800) 669-8387
	(404) 657-5334
HAWAII	(808) 586-0100
IDAHO	S.W. (800) 247-4422
	(208) 334-4250
	North (800) 488-5725
	(208) 799-5075
	S.E. (800) 488-5764
	(208) 236-6044
	Cent. (800) 488-5731
	(208) 736-4713
ILLINOIS	(800) 548-9034
	(217) 785-9021
INDIANA	(800) 452-4800
	(317) 233-3475
	(317) 232-5299
IOWA	(800) 351-4664
	(515) 281-5705
KANSAS	(800) 432-3535
	(913) 296-4986
KENTUCKY	(800) 564-7372
LOUISIANA	(800) 259-5301
MAINE	(800) 750-5353
	(207) 623-1797
MARYLAND	(800) 243-3425
	(410) 767-1074
MASSACHUSETTS	(800) 882-2003
	(504) 342-5301
	(617) 727-7750

STATE INSURANCE COUNSELING (cont.)

STATE	PHONE NUMBER
MICHIGAN	(800) 803-7174
MINNESOTA	(800) 882-6262
	(612) 296-2770
MISSISSIPPI	(800) 948-3090
	(601) 359-4951
MISSOURI	(800) 390-3330
	(573) 893-7900
MONTANA	(800) 332-2272
NEBRASKA	(402) 471-2201
NEVADA	(800) 307-4444
	(702) 486-4602
NEW HAMPSHIRE	(800) 852-3388
	(605) 225-9000
NEW JERSEY	(800) 792-8820
NEW MEXICO	(800) 432-2080
	(505) 827-7640
NEW YORK	(800) 333-4114
	(212) 869-3850 (NY City Area)
NORTH CAROLINA	(800) 443-9354
NORTH DAKOTA	(800) 247-0560
	(701) 328-2440
OKLAHOMA	(800) 763-2828
	(405) 521-6628
OREGON	(800) 722-4134
	(503) 378-4636, Ext. 600
PENNSYLVANIA	(800) 783-7067
OHIO	(800) 686-1578
	(614) 644-3458
PUERTO RICO	(809) 721-5710

STATE INSURANCE COUNSELING (cont.)

STATE	PHONE NUMBER
RHODE ISLAND	(800) 322-2880
	(401) 277-2880
SOUTH CAROLINA	(800) 868-9095
	(803) 737-7500
SOUTH DAKOTA	(605) 773-3656
TENNESSEE	(800) 525-2816
TEXAS	(800) 252-3439
UTAH	(801) 538-3910
VERMONT	(800) 250-8472
	(802) 861-1577
VIRGIN ISLANDS	(809) 774-2991, Ext. 248
	(809) 774-7166, Ext. 248
VIRGINIA	(800) 552-3402
WASHINGTON	(800) 605-6299
WEST VIRGINIA	(304) 558-3317
WISCONSIN	(800) 242-1060
WYOMING	(800) 856-4398
	(307) 856-6880

APPENDIX G

With the choices of coverage for Medicare beneficiaries expanding in sometimes dizzying ways, there are a number of places for older Americans to turn for help in addition to state insurance hot lines. The American Association of Retired Persons can be reached at 202-434-2277. The organization's address is 601 E Street NW, Washington, DC 20049. Another good resource is the Medicare Rights Center, 212-869-3850, at 1460 Broadway, New York, New York 10036. By late 1998, the Federal government is planning to establish a web site (www.medicarehelp.gov), which will list available Medicare options by location and provide other information. In addition, there are Federally financed organizations across the country whose mandate is to help older Americans with their insurance decisions. A good starting point for you is your state agency on aging.

APPENDIX G

HELP FOR OLDER AMERICANS

Commission on Aging
770 Washington Avenue, Suite 470
P.O. Box 301851
Montgomery, AL 36130
(800) 243-5463
(334) 242-5594

Division of Senior Services
3601 C Street, Suite 310
Anchorage, AK 99503
(907) 563-5654

Division of Aging and Adult Services
1417 Donaghey Plaza South
P.O. Box 1437, Slot 1412
Little Rock, AR 72203-1437
(501) 682-2441

Department of Economic Security
Aging and Adult Administration
1789 West Jefferson Street
Phoenix, AZ 85007
(602) 542-4446

Department of Aging
Health Insurance, Counseling and Advocacy Branch
1600 K Street
Sacramento, CA 95814
Phone: (916) 322-3887
Fax: (916) 324-1903

APPENDIX G

Aging and Adult Services
Department of Human Services
110 Sixteenth Street
Suite 200
Denver, CO 80203-1714
(303) 620-4147

Connecticut Commission on Aging
25 Sigourney Street
Hartford, CT 06106-5033
(860) 424-5360

Office on Aging
441 Fourth Street, NW
Ninth Floor
Washington, DC 20001
(202) 724-5626
(202) 724-5622

Services for Aging and Adults with Physical Disabilities
Department of Health and Social Services
1901 North Dupont Highway
Second Floor Annex Administration Building
New Castle, DE 19720
(800) 223-9074
(302) 577-4791

Department of Elder Affairs
4040 Esplanade Way, Suite 260
Tallahassee, FL 32399-7000
(800) 96ELDER
(904) 414-2060

APPENDIX G

Division of Aging Services
Department of Human Resources
2 Peachtree Street NW Room 36-385
Atlanta, GA 30303
(404) 657-5258

Executive Office on Aging
250 South Hotel Street
Suite 107
Honolulu, HI 96813
(808) 586-0100

Department of Elder Affairs
200 Tenth Street, Third Floor
Des Moines, IA 50309-3709
(515) 281-5187

Office on Aging
Statehouse, Room 108
Boise, ID 83720
(208) 334-3833

Department on Aging
421 East Capitol Avenue, #100
Springfield, IL 62701-1789
(800) 252-8966

Division on Aging and Home Services
402 West Washington Street
P.O. Box 7083
Indianapolis, IN 46207-7083
(800) 545-7763
(317) 232-7020

APPENDIX G

Department on Aging
150 South Docking State Office Building
915 SW Harrison
Topeka, KS 66612-1500
(913) 296-4986

Division of Aging Services
Cabinet of Family and Children
275 East Main Street
Frankfort, KY 40621
(502) 564-7372

Governor's Office of Elderly Affairs
4550 North Boulevard
P.O. Box 80374
Baton Rouge, LA 70806-0374
(504) 925-1700

Bureau of Elder and Adult Services
State House, Station 11
Augusta, ME 04333
(207) 624-5335

Office on Aging
301 West Preston Street
Room 1007
Baltimore, MD 21201
(410) 767-1074

Office of Services to the Aging
611 West Ottawa Street
P.O. Box 30026

Lansing, MI 48909
(517) 373-8230

Board on Aging
Human Services Building, Fourth Floor
444 Lafayette Road
St. Paul, MN 55155-3843
(612) 296-2770

Division of Aging and Adult Services
750 North State Street
Jackson, MS 39202
(800) 948-3090
(601) 359-4929

Division of Aging
Department of Social Services
P.O. Box 1337
615 Howeton Court
Jefferson City, MO 65109-1337
(800) 235-5503
(573) 751-3082

Division of Senior and Long-Term Care/DPHHS
P.O. Box 4210
Helena, MT 59604-4210
(800) 332-2272
(406) 444-7781

Department of Aging
State Office Building

APPENDIX G

301 Centennial Mall South
Lincoln, NE 68509-5044
(800) 942-7830
(402) 471-2306

Department of Human Resources
Division for Aging Services
340 North Eleventh Street, Suite 114
Las Vegas, NV 89101
(800) 243-3638
(702) 486-3545

Department of Health & Human Services
Division of Elderly & Adult Services
State Office Park South
115 Pleasant Street
Annex Building No. 1
Concord, NH 03301
(603) 271-4680

Department of Community Affairs
Division on Aging
101 South Broad Street
CN 807
Trenton, NJ 08625-0807
(800) 792-8820
(609) 984-3951

State Agency on Aging
La Villa Rivera Building
224 East Palace Avenue

APPENDIX G

Santa Fe, NM 87501
(800) 432-2080
(505) 827-7640

State Office for the Aging
2 Empire State Plaza
Albany, NY 12223-0001
(800) 342-9871
(518) 474-9871

Division of Aging
693 Palmer Drive
Caller Box 29531
Raleigh, NC 27626-0531
(919) 733-3983

Department of Human Services
Aging Services Division
P.O. Box 7070
Bismarck, ND 58507-7070
(701) 328-8910

Department of Aging
50 West Broad Street, Ninth Floor
Columbus, OH 43215-5928
(800) 282-1206
(614) 466-1221

Department of Human Services
Aging Services Division
312 NE Twenty-eighth Street
Oklahoma City, OK 73125
(405) 521-2327

APPENDIX G

Department of Human Resources
Senior and Disabled Services Division
500 Summer Street NE
Second Floor
Salem, OR 97310-1015
(800) 232-3020
(503) 945-5811

Department of Aging
"APPRISE" Health Insurance Counseling
and Assistance
400 Market Street
Rachel Carson State Office Building
Harrisburg, PA 17101
(800) 783-7067

Governor's Office of Elderly Affairs
Gericulture Commission
Box 11398
Santurce, PR 00910
(809) 722-2429

Department of Elderly Affairs
160 Pine Street
Providence, RI 02903
(401) 277-2858

Division on Aging
202 Arbor Lake Drive
Suite 301
Columbia, SC 29223-4554
(803) 737-7500

APPENDIX G

Office of Adult Services and Aging
700 Governors Drive
Pierre, SD 57501-2291
(605) 773-3656

Commission on Aging
Andrew Jackson Building
Ninth Floor
500 Deaderick Street
Nashville, TN 37243
(615) 741-2056

Department of Aging
P.O. Box 12786 (78711)
1949 IH 35 South
Austin, TX 78741
(800) 252-9240
(512) 424-6840

Division of Aging and Adult Services
120 North 200 West
Salt Lake City, UT 84103
(801) 538-3910

Department of Aging and Disabilities
Waterbury Complex
103 South Main Street
Waterbury, VT 05671-2301
(802) 241-2400

Department of the Aging
1600 Forest Avenue
Richmond, VA 23229

APPENDIX G

(800) 552-3402
(804) 662-9333

Aging and Adult Services Administration
Department of Social and Health Services
P.O. Box 45600
Olympia, WA 98504-5600
(360) 493-2500

Commission on Aging
State Capitol Complex
Holly Grove
1900 Kanawha Boulevard East
Charleston, WV 25305-0160
(304) 558-3317

Board on Aging and Long-Term Care
214 North Hamilton Street
Madison, WI 53703
(800) 242-1060
(608) 266-8944

Division on Aging
Hathaway Building
2300 Capitol Avenue
Room 139
Cheyenne, WY 82002
(800) 442-2766
(307) 777-7986

Index

Abortion, 77
Accreditation, 26–27
   chart, 173–88
   denied, 174
   full, 173
   one-year, 173
   provisional, 174
Acupuncture, 41
Aetna, 65, 166
After-birth services, 70
AIDS, 42–43, 112, 120, 123–29
   and case management, 123–26
   and doctors, 127–28
   and drugs, 132, 134
   and getting into plan, 128–29
Alternative therapies, 41
American Association of Retired Persons (AARP), 105, 265
American Board of Medical Specialties, 29
American Cancer Society, 128
American College of Emergency Physicians, 136
American Diabetes Association, 128
American Health Information Management Association, 148
American Heart Association, 118

Angioplasty rates, 127
Annual caps, 134
Annual checkups, 102
Annual physicals, 30, 36
Appeals, 154, 155–64
   board, 161
   mental health coverage, 141–42
   notice, filing, 159–60
   process, 56, 119, 126, 160–61
Appointments, 24, 35–36
Arthritis, 110, 111–12, 116
Artificial insemination, 71
As Good As It Gets (film), xiii
Asthma, 110, 112
   and children, 81–82
   and home visits, 115–16
Avmed plan (Florida), 65

Benchmark plans, 249–50
Beta blockers, 127, 175
Bills
   keeping copies of, 169–70
   not paid on time, 3
Birthing classes, 70
Blue Cross/Blue Shield, 2, 3
   of California, 112
   of Northeastern New York, 7–8, 13

INDEX

Selections HMO, 53
of Western New York, 67
Board certification, 29, 55
Bone marrow transplants, 53, 118, 154, 156
Breast cancer
screening, 63, 64, 174–75
treatment, 71, 121–23
Bypass operations, 127

Cain, Christopher, 91–93
Cain, Dean, 93
Cancer, 34, 53, 63, 71, 106–7, 120
drugs for, 132
and insurance, 129
and treatment, 121–23, 131
Capitation fee
defined, 17, 25–26
problems with, 26, 58
and specialists, 127
Carve-out companies, 42, 140–45
and privacy, 146–47
and treatment options, 150–51
Case management
and appeals, 161–62
and chronic illness, 111, 112, 115–17
and major illness, 41, 121–23, 125–28, 130–31
Caseworkers, and privacy, 147–49
Cason family, 4–9, 12
Catastrophic coverage policy, 51
Center for the Study of Services, 27–28
Cervical cancer, 65, 71
Cesarean delivery rates, 66–67, 70

Chemotherapy, 122–23, 154, 156
Chest pains, 36
Childbirth
and cesarean delivery, 66–67
and coverage for child, 74
evaluating coverage for, 69–70
and hospital stays, 55, 63, 65–66
and midwives, 62–63
Children, 72–76, 78, 83–84
and chronic conditions, 80–82, 115
college-age, 82–83
and immunizations, 79
Chiropractor, 53
Choice, xii, 12
and mental health services, 150
and point-of-service plans, 5–6
Cholesterol screening, 30, 127
Christian Fidelity Life medigap, 104
Chronic illness, 13, 34, 108–19
and children, 80–82, 84
and Medicare, 96
and specialist as primary care physician, 39
Cigna company, 64, 65–66, 68, 79, 127
Clinton, Bill, 63
COBRA (1983), 47, 75, 83
Colitis, 118
College students, 82–83
Collins, Mary, 72–74, 77
Colon cancer screening, 30
Community organizations, 144
Comparison charts, 12–13
Complaints
and Families USA, 242

| 278 |

INDEX

and mental health services, 140
and state insurance departments, 27, 57
Conn, Dr. Doyt, 111, 116
Consumers, 15
Contact person, 127
Contract, 160, 167
Convenience, 35–38
Co-payment
    and childbirth, 70
    and comparing costs, 6, 32, 33–34
    defined, 2, 15
    and dual policies, 76–77
    and fee-for-service, 2, 15
    and HMOs, 50, 76
    and maximum limits, 32–33
    and Medicare HMO, 87, 101
    point of service, 5, 18
Corporate health policy consortiums, 28
Costs, ix, 24, 31–34
    deductibles and co-payments vs. premiums, 2, 6, 32–34
    and HMOs, 50
    and maximum limits, 32, 34
    and Medicare HMOs, 101
Courts, 162–63
Coverage
    evaluating with cost, 32
    limits on maximum costs, 32–33
    see also Denial of coverage
Covered life, 16
Coworkers, 24–25
Crohn's disease, 118
Cutting-edge treatments, 53

and chronic illness, 118–19
and denial of coverage, 53, 155–64
drugs, 117, 132
and major illness, 121
and Medicare, 100–101

D'Amato, Alfonse, 156
Deductible
    banking premium, 8
    defined, 1, 2, 15
    fee-for-service, 15, 51
    and HMOs, 50, 76
    vs. other costs, 32, 33–34
    point-of-service options, 18
    vs. premiums, 6, 7–8, 13
Denial of coverage, 56
    appeals procedure, 119
    and chronic illness, 118–19
    how to fight, 153–65, 170
    and mental health hospitalization, 141–42
    see also Appeals
Dental coverage, 44
Dependents, 75–76
Depression, 145
Diabetes, 109–10, 175
    kits, 32, 110
Disability coverage, 44–45
Disaster policy, 51
Discrimination, 106–7, 130
Divorce, 148
Doctor
    and appeals, 161–62
    availability of, 7, 12, 35, 58
    bonuses to, 58

INDEX

choice of, 2–3, 17–18
compensation methods, 17, 25–26, 58, 89, 98
evaluating, 6, 29, 57–58
female, 69
and gag rules, xii
and information on coverage, 25, 169
and late payments, 56, 58
and major illness, 125, 127–28
and Medicare, 89, 98
and Medicare HMO, 85, 90–96
and payment limits, 32–33
and provider sponsored organizations, 97
proximity of, 6–7, 12
relationship with, 17
and staff vs. group model HMO, 20–21
see also Primary care physician; Specialist
Drugstore, 36
Dual coverage, 74–77, 83

Egg implantation, 71
Emergency room, 36–37
and asthma, 31, 81
calling for approval, 166
and major illness, 135–36
and Medicare HMOs, 100
and travel, 38
Employee assistance programs, 143–44
Employer, 9–11
as information resource, 28, 29, 31, 168–69
and mental health records, 148
rebates, 73–74
Employer-funded plans
and appeals, 163
and mental health coverage, 149
and state regulation, 37
Epidurals, 70
ER (TV show), xiii
Exclusive Health Care (Dallas), 64
Expedited review, 159
"Experimental" treatments, 53, 100, 118, 134–35.
see also Cutting-edge treatments

Families
and children, 72–76, 83–84
and fertility and pregnancy, 77–80
Families USA, 159, 160
Medicare HMO survey, 241–48
website and phone, 242
Family doctor, 5
Family medical history, 13
Federal government, 37
health care legislation, 242
member survey, 30, 211–40
Fee-for-service policy
cost of, 2
defined, 1–2, 15
and high deductible, 51, 53–54
and mental health coverage, 152
Fertility treatments, 53, 70–71, 77–78
FHP International, 91–93
Fibroids, 68
Financial management, 24, 56

| 280 |

INDEX

First Priority HMO (Northeast Pennsylvania), 67
Fixed fees, 17
Flexibility, 38–39
Flexible spending accounts, 46–47
Florida, 162
Flu shots, 30, 33
Food and Drug Administration, 21, 117, 132
Formulary
   and chronic illness, 117
   defined, 21
   HMO, 51, 59
   and major illness, 126, 128, 132
   and mental health, 150
For-profit plans, 19
Foundation Health of California, 68
Fox, Peter D., 114, 168
Friends, 24–25, 164

Gag rules, xii, 25
"Gatekeeper"
   avoiding plan with, 11
   defined, x–xi
   and women, 63
   see also primary care physician
Gay Men's Health Crisis, 133
General Motors, 28, 35, 249–50
Generic drugs, 21, 41, 117, 150
Genetic testing, 123
Gibbs, Linda, 153–56, 161, 162, 164
Grannis, Pete, 156–57
Green, Mark, 165
Greineder, Dr. Dirk K., 82
Group Health Cooperative of Eau Claire, 80

Group Health Cooperative of Puget Sound, 19–20, 79
Group Health Northwest (Seattle), 64
Group therapy, 42, 144
GTE, 28
"Guarantee issue" laws, 113
Gulf South Health Plans (New Orleans), 65

Halverson, George, 132
Hamilton, Elaine, 161, 163–64
Harvard Community Health Plan, 61, 68
Harvard Pilgrim plan, 19, 81–82
Health care
   changes in, ix–x
   costs, ix, xii, xiii, 2, 6, 31–34, 50, 101
   and primary concerns, 22–47
   terminology, 14–21
Health Care Financing Administration, 118
Health care plan
   basic options, 1–4
   and chronically ill, 108–19
   evaluating, 24–47
   and families with children, 72–76, 78, 80–84
   file, keeping, 167–68
   leaving unsatisfactory, 170–71
   and major illness, 120–36
   and married couples, 73–77, 83
   and mental health needs, 137–52
   and patient rights, 153–65
   phone representatives, 165–66

INDEX

researching, 4–13
resources for evaluating, 24–28
and senior citizens, 85–107
and women, 61–71
and young singles, 48–60
Health Cooperative of Puget Sound, 127–28
Health Insurance Plan (HIP, New York), 68, 165
Health maintenance organizations (HMOs)
  capitation fees, 58
  and choice, xii, 5
  and co-payment comparisons, 33
  cost of, 2
  defined, x–xi, 16–18
  Families USA survey of, 241–48
  Federal survey of, 213–36
  for-profit vs. not-for profit, 19
  group vs. staff model, 20
  and hospital care, 54–55
  restrictions of, 51–60
  simplicity of, 37, 50–51
  state regulators, 251–59
  steps for analyzing, 52–60
  and young, single people, 49–60
  see also Medicare HMO, 88
HealthNet (California), 149
HealthNet HMO (Empire Blue Cross and Blue Shield), 27
Health New England, 68
Health Pages, 27, 103
HealthPartners (Minnesota), 132
Heart attack, 106, 127

Heart disease, 34, 120, 126–27, 129, 132, 175
Hemy, Nadine, 93–95
Henry J. Kaiser Foundation, xiii
Hewlett-Packard, 151
HIV, 42–43, 123
  see also AIDS
HMO Group, 145
Holistic medicine, 41
Home care, 32, 101, 102
Home visits, 115–16
Hospital
  annual and lifetime caps on, 34, 41, 134
  and childbirth, xii, 63, 65–66, 70, 175–76
  choice of, 5
  and chronic illness, 116
  coverage, comparing, 55
  and information on coverage, 169
  and Medicare HMO, 85, 87
  and Medicare, traditional, 86
  and mental health problems, 141–42
  and provider sponsored organizations, 97
  quality of, 29–30
  referral for HMO, 16–17
  and special needs, 41
  stays minimized, xii, 54–55, 65–66
  teaching, 29–30
  and travel, 38
  see also Emergency room
Hybrid plans, xii–xiii
Hysterectomy, 67–68, 71

| 282 |

INDEX

Illinois, 161
Immunizations, 79, 84, 174
Independent review panels, 158, 170
Individual coverage, 4–9
Individual practice associations, 20–21
Infertility tests, 77
Information
 and phone representatives, 165–71
 resources, 24–28
Insulin, 109–10
In vitro fertilization, 77
Is Your Health Information Confidential?, 149

Job, leaving
 and COBRA, 47
 and dual vs. single coverage, 75
 and preexisting conditions, 40–41
Johnson, Bill, 72–74, 77
Joint replacement, 116

Kaiser of Southern California, 49, 87, 101
Kaiser Permanente, 19, 20, 163
Kamarowski, Shirley, 62
Kennedy-Kassebaum health care bill (1996), 40–41, 75, 113
Kings County Blue Cross Blue Shield, 53
Kitts, Joan, 108–10, 117

Large companies, employee satisfaction polls, 57
Lawyer, 162, 163

Lifetime ceilings, 134
Livesley, Lynn, 79
Location
 of doctors and hospitals, 24
 of drugstore, 36
Long-term care, 45–46, 104–6
Lynch, Marianne, 68–69

Major illnesses, 120–36
Mammograms, 30, 63, 102
Managed care
 and AIDS, 124–25
 benefits of, xiii–xiv
 and chronically ill, 108–11
 cost of premiums, xiii, 2–3
 defined, x, 2–3, 15–16
 dissatisfaction with, xiii
 fixed fees to doctors, xi–xii
 growth of, x, 15
 management problems, xi, 3–4, 56
 and mental health needs, 138–39
 reform bills, 158
 researching options, 4–11
 savings created by, xi
 types of, x–xi, 16–21
 see also Health maintenance organization; Point of service plans; Preferred provider organizations
Married couples, 73–77
Massachusetts, 113
Massachusetts Blue Cross, 147
Mastectomies, xii
 and gatekeeper, 63
 and hospital stays, 55
 rates, 71

| 283 |

INDEX

Maternity coverage, 44, 70
   vs. coverage for children, 78
   hospital stay, 175–76
   see also Childbirth; Pregnancy
MDNY Health Care (New York), 65
Medicaid
   and major illness, 129–30
   and nursing home, 104
Medical devices, 117
Medical equipment, 32, 101
Medical forms, 5
Medical savings accounts, 88–89, 97–98
Medicare, 85–107
   advantages of traditional, 95
   and co-payments, 88
   costs of traditional, 86–87
   and medical savings account, 97–98
   and provider sponsored organizations, 97
   regulations, 107, 134
   threats to, 90, 96, 102
   website, 98
   where to get help, 265–75
Medicare HMOs, 85–90, 98
   costs, 101
   denial of quality care by, 91–96
   discrimination against older and sicker, 106–7
   evaluating, 99–107
   Families USA survey, 241–48
   and restrictions on doctors, 90–96
Medicare Rights Center, 265
Medigap, 86–87, 88, 94, 95

cost of, 96, 102–3
evaluating plans, 102–4
Membership benefits package, 160–61, 167–68
Member surveys, 30
   Families USA, 241–48
   federal, 211–40
Mental health services, 137–52
   and evaluating plan, 13, 42
   options outside plan, 143–44
   subcontractors, 42
   see also Carve-out companies
MetraHealth, 108–11
Mid-Hudson Health Plan, 2
Midwives, 62, 63, 70
Missouri, 160
Moynihan, Daniel Patrick, 156

National Association of Insurance Commissioners, 105
National Coalition of Mental Health Consumers and Professionals, 151
National Commission on Quality Assurance (NCQA), 26–27, 30, 31, 64, 67, 79, 80
   accreditation chart, 173–87
   quality chart, 174–76, 188–210
   website and phone number, 27, 174
Needham, Christine, 61–63
Network, defined, 21
New Jersey, 113
New York State, 113, 129, 131–32
   managed care bill of rights, 156
Nonmedical employees, 133

INDEX

North Carolina, 159
Not-for-profit plans, 19–20, 144
Nurse practitioners, 29
Nutritionist, 110
NYLCare Health Plans, 27, 65

Obstetrician-gynecologist, 39, 63, 69–70
Oncologist, 63
Ovarian cancer, 153–54, 156
Oxford company, 35, 157, 164
   and denial of care, 154, 155–56
   financial problems, 56
   Freedom plan, 125, 128
   Freedom vs. Liberty plans, 35

PacifiCare, 92–93
Pacific Business Group on Health, 28, 57
Panel
   and childbirth, 70
   defined, 16
   different, in same company, 35
   evaluating, 55–56
   and Medicare HMO, 99–100
Panzarino, Dr. Peter, 150–51
Pap smears, 30, 63, 65
Parks, Cindy, 137–38, 150, 152
Patient rights, 153–64
Pediatrician, 78, 84
Per visit payment, 25
Phone help lines, 24, 37, 167, 169–70
Physical therapists, 41, 116
Physician's assistants, 29
Physicians Mutual medigap, 103–4

Plan member, defined, 16
Point-of-service plans (POS)
   comparing costs, 32, 33–34
   defined, 5, 18
   federal survey of, 237–40
   and major illness, 128
   and mental health services, 145–46, 150
   and record-keeping, 169
Policyholder, 16
Politicians, 164
Pool insurance plans, 113, 129
Preexisting conditions
   and chronic illnesses, 113
   and evaluating plan, 40–41
   and getting into plan, 128–30
Preferred provider organizations, 5, 18–19
Pregnancy, 44, 62–63, 69–71, 77–80. *see also* Childbirth; Maternity coverage
Premium
   comparing, 31
   vs. deductibles, 6, 7–8
   defined, 2, 15
   fee-for-service, 2, 15
   managed care, 2, 3
   for married couples, 73, 74
   and state pool, 113, 129
Prenatal appointments, 70
Prescription drugs
   annual and lifetime caps on, 134
   approved list of, 21
   and childbirth, 70
   and chronic illness, 117
   co-payments, 2

INDEX

denial of coverage, 36, 122–23
and evaluating cost of plan, 32
and major illness, 121–22, 126, 132
and Medicare HMO, 87, 94, 95, 101
and mental health needs, 139, 141, 150
and special needs, 41, 59, 109–10
see also Formulary
Preventive care, 3
and children, 78–79
evaluating, 30–31, 63–64
and Medicare HMO, 102
Primary care doctors
availability of, 35
avoiding, 19
and board certification, 29
and capitation fees, xi, 26
choosing, 57–58
and chronic illness, 114–15, 131
defined, 16
and depression, 145
location of, 6–7
and referrals, 26, 51
restrictions on, 53–54
and rights, 153–54
specialist as, 38–39, 131–32
switching, 38
for women, 63
Privacy, 146–49
Protease inhibitor, 126, 128
Protocol of best treatment, 130
Provider, 15
Provider sponsored organizations, 97
Prozac, 141

Prudential, 67, 68, 169
"Prudent layperson" standard, 36, 136
Psychiatrist, 141
Psychologist, 141
Psychotherapy co-payments, 142

Quality of care, 23, 29–31
and doctors, 55–56
and Medicare HMOs, 91–96

Ratings
agencies, 23, 26–26, 29
large companies, 57
"Reasonable and customary charge," 32, 33
Rebates, 59–60, 73–74
Record-keeping, 167–71
Referrals
and chronic illness, 109, 112
ease of, 58
and major illness, 131
multiple, 39, 55
see also Specialists
Reimbursement
process, 37–38
and record keeping, 169–70
see also Denial of coverage
Religious organizations, 144
Routine checkups, 33, 35–36

Sanders, Steve, 156
Scherzer, Mark, 156
Second opinions, 38
Self-employed, 4–9
Self-funded plans, 37

INDEX

Senior citizens, 85–107
    resources for, 265–75
Shore, Dr. Karen, 151
Small business, 4–9, 61
Social worker, 141
Special health needs, 40–43
Specialist
    access to, 41, 54
    and board certification, 29, 55
    and choice, 5
    and chronic illness, 109, 112, 114–17
    and HMO, 16–18
    location of, 6
    and major illness, 125, 131–32
    and Medicare HMO, 91–96
    as primary care physician, 26, 38–39, 112–13, 131–32
    and rights, 153–54
    seeing, without referral, 11, 12, 19, 39
    see also Referrals
Special treatment programs, 31
"Spending down" assets, 104
Staley, Peter, 124–26, 128, 133
Standard Life & Accident medigap, 104
State agencies, 23, 29, 31
    on aging, 265
    regulating HMOs, 251–59
State insurance department, 27, 31, 37–38, 55, 56, 162
    hotlines, 261–64
State regulation, 35–37, 63, 129, 131, 242
    and appeals, 159–62

Stem cell transplants, 156
Sterilization, 77
Stewart family, 1–4, 12
Storch, Audrey and Michael, 121–23, 128
Surgery, 54–55

Talk therapy, 139–40, 141
Taylor, Dr. John, 79
Teams, 112, 131–32
Terminology, 14–21
Tests, free, 63–65, 69
Therapy, 123, 137–52
    application, 146–48
    choice of therapist, 122
    number of visits, 42, 149–50
    objectives, 150–52
Thomas, Bill, 128
Thomas, George, 91–93
Thompson, Ralph, 85–87, 89, 101
Timbers family, 9–11
Traumatic brain injury, 94
Travel, 38
Travelers Insurance, 166
Treatment Action Group, 124–25
Treatment coordination, 121–23, 133–34

United American Health Care medigap, 103–4
United Health Care of Minnesota, 112
U.S. Congress, xii, 97, 158, 163
U.S. Healthcare, 166
U.S. News & World Report, 30
"Urgent care situations," 159

INDEX

Urgent conditions, appointments for, 35
US Healthcare Medicare HMO, 93–94
Utilization review officers, 148

Vermont, 160
Virginia, 160
Virginia Mason plan, 66
Vision and eyeglass coverage, 44, 175
  and Medicare HMO, 87, 94, 101, 103
Vista Health Plans, 150

Wall Street Journal, The, 150
Washington Business Group on Health, 28

Washington state, 113
Web sites, 27, 28, 98, 174, 242, 265
Welcome kits, 117
Well baby and child visits, 30, 79, 80, 84
Well Care, 3, 4
Wisconsin, 159
Wojnowski, Chuck, 48–51, 54, 55
Wolfson, Dan, 145
Women, 45, 61–71, 175

Young, single people, 48–60
Your Health Information Belongs to You, 148–49